1

Acronym Preacher has something in each of the chapters that will be a blessing in your life. God has placed an anointing on the author, Dr. Cindy Bailey that allows her to connect with His people all over. This book is empowering for individuals and ministries.

Pastor Tanya Brown
Wings of Prayer Ministry Inc.

Acronym Preacher is like meeting the Author Dr. Cindy Bailey. It is a never-to-be-forgotten experience; it leaves an indelible mark upon every life that it/she touches.
The book, like the author has a heart and vision to equip believers to fulfill their divine destiny.

Apostle Dr. Gloria Holden, Chancellor
Fellowship International School of Ministry and Bible College

ACRONYM
PREACHER

DR. CINDY BAILEY

DEDICATION

Father God,

I Thank You Lord, that you are my Joy and my Strength. I seek ye first the kingdom of God and your righteousness, that all things will be added unto thee!

I would like to dedicate this book to my twelve (12) G.E.N.I.U.S **G (God's) E(exceptional) N(novas) I(incredible) U(unique) S(savvy)** grandchildren as I name you one by one: Pierre Garmon, Xavier Khaalid, Kennedi Bailey, Amani Godfrey, Zierre Khaalid, Daejha Godfrey, Lyla Bailey, Eryin Collins, Millie Bailey, Evin Collins, Andrea Ellis & Charles Ellis. You are my bright and morning stars. All of you are so gifted, talented, creative and knowledgeable and can be whatever you want to be! I pray purpose and prosperity over each of your lives. You can do all things through Christ who gives you strength!

To my children: Sa'D Matt Khaalid, R'Iana Siobhan Bailey, DiJonElla Luvy Collins, and Kaz Andre Bailey, thank you for being the Best Godly Parents to my Genius Grandchildren. Thank you for your different personalities, strong wills and unique sibling love for each other.

Saving the best for last; I am grateful to my loving, awesome, Godly husband and BFF, Anthon Bailey (My Boo) for always supporting me and encouraging me in Ministry. You complete me. I Love you for Life and I Thank God for HIM choosing Me for You! *#Life with You is 2 Good + 2 EverBe= 4Gotten!*

ACKNOWLEDGMENTS

To My Lord and Savior, Jesus Christ, I give you all the praise, honor and glory. You created and molded me and gave me gifts, skills and talents which allowed me to write this book.

I thank my deceased parents, Jules and Diane Harvey, who adopted me, raised me and loved me. You were always there for me and my children, Matt and Luvy, through the good and the bad. Words can't express how I miss the both of you. I am so sorry for the pain that I caused both of you (by being rebellious); when I learned I was adopted. At that age, I didn't understand that you saved my life. I wouldn't be here if it weren't for the both of you! See you in Heaven!

I thank the Holy Spirit, who showed up and showed out in full power in the prayer and spoke accurately in the prophetic on May 13th @ 7pm at Embellish Salons on Stewart Mill Pkwy, Douglasville, GA 30135. When you said, **"It's T.I.M.E"** (Trust In Me Entirely) the book that had been in the womb for 25 months was now in delivery stage for birth. I whole heartedly thank Ms. Odessia Brewer (owner/operator) of Embellish Salon for her strong anointing and obedience to the Holy Spirit to request HIS presence in prayer.

I am so humbly grateful to Dr. Gloria Holden (Spiritual Mother & Chancellor of Fellowship International School of Ministry and Bible College, Metairie, LA) and Apostle Frances Collins (Mentor & Pastor of New Beginning Women's Ministry, Stockbridge, GA (NBWM). These two (2) mighty women of God are the pillars in my life. They hold my arms up when I am weak and keep me on the straight and narrow. They expose the 'Me' that I don't see, they continually impart wisdom and knowledge, they expand my faith with vision assignments and most of ALL they cover me in Prayer! I love, respect and appreciate them to infiniti!

I sincerely appreciate and thank my leader, Bishop Dr. David E Jackson, who keeps it 110 with me, who preaches and teaches true Gospel from the Word of God. You train and push me to the next level in Ministry. You share immeasurably your experience, knowledge, skills, time and above all, your love to me and everyone in the kingdom. I am honored to be your Marketing PR of DE Jackson Enterprise and a leader under ADP lineage! (Apostolic Petrine Disciple) I pray prodigious Jabez Blessings over every area in your life.

I give major thanks to my Sister, Prophetess Etoyi Billings (GEM Transportation, Douglasville, GA) and my Sister, Pastor Tanya Brown (Wings of Prayer Ministry, Waltersboro, SC) All my life Being adopted, I grew up an only child. I have considered many women in my life to be my Sisters in Christ, but when God placed you both in my life for different longevity seasons, I praised him because I was no longer the only child. Although spending time in person is always best, it doesn't matter if it's five minutes or fifty minutes, whether we have a verbal conversation or text, Iron Sharpens Iron! The intercession is an empowering divine connection and the Joy, Laughter, and Love is REAL! I decree the divine favor of God for each of your every heart's desire.

I thank my friends, colleagues, my Mt. Sinai Family, my many Presbyter Brothers & Sisters of the Gospel throughout the world for your encouragement, prayers and allowing me to be ME! I know I took some getting used to (always laughing, smiling, going like the energizer bunny) but it's your LOVE, it's your heart for the Kingdom and being about Our Father's business that fuels me. Thank you for allowing me to be a vessel in your life and your ministry, whenever there's a need, I am honored to be there to serve.

I exceedingly thank my editor, as well as Coach Kurinn Wright, (Coach Wright Consulting) and Mr. Mark Emerson, my graphic designer (Mr. E Films). This dynamic team are the stupendous doctors that delivered my baby! Your expertise, your patience and charisma is truly astounding. Like a three strand cord, Ecclesiastes 4:12-And if one prevail against him, two shall withstand him; and a threefold chord is not quickly broken. I'm eagerly waiting for the birth of the other babies to come!

Peace & Blessings
Rev Dr. Cindy Bailey
Acronym Preacher

FOREWORD

As a child, I learned quickly that one of the greatest gifts I could have was the ability to dream! The reason why dreams are so important, especially when you are a child, is that it helps you see all the possibilities that life holds for you. It takes you beyond the here and now to see that you can have, be and do whatever you want to do in life, despite what you may see around you. Dreams play a greater role in our lives. Dreams can give us clues about what our purpose in life is, especially those reoccurring ones. Those dreams begin to connect to the gifts and talents we have inside of us and from that, we begin to answer one of the biggest questions in our lives: WHY IN THE WORLD AM I ALIVE?

That is what purpose is all about: figuring out what we are in the Earth to do. You and I are alive for a purpose and if we do not identify that purpose early, we will become convinced that we are here merely for breathing and existing. Let me declare to you that your life's purpose is much bigger than being popular. It is greater than being famous or obtaining a lot of things. Once you discover what that thing is, the one thing you are here to do that no one can do like you, then you will start the journey of living on purpose! The earlier you figure out what that thing IS, then the faster and smoother you will move into destiny! WHY? Because once you have figured out your life's purpose, everything in your life must have something to do with getting you closer to it. Your decisions, your friends, your performance in your career and your behavior all must center around purpose. That means that when people, places and things come up in your life that may keep you from getting closer to purpose or mess up your destiny, then you have to make a decision to SAY NO TO THAT THING AND SAY YES TO PURPOSE!

It requires you to take ownership of your life, the decisions you make and the path you take when setting out towards purpose! One of my favorite TV shows as a kid was a show with a game that had three doors. Behind each door were different prizes and opportunities that would take the person down different paths. Each door had its own specific key that was cut to fit the lock on that particular door; however, THE CHOICE, THE OPTION was in the hands of the participant! The participant had to make a choice as to which door and which path would take them closer to where they wanted to go.

Just like those participants, you too have the keys and you must decide which door, which path and which option is going to get you closer to your purpose. Life is a journey and only you hold the key to it! And the question is what are you going to do with it? Well Cindy Bailey has taken the keys of her purpose and has used them to produce this wonderful book. Dr. Bailey's gift of acronyms in her messages has empowered men and women to walk in their assignment and calling in God. Her uncanny ability to communicate a Rhema word to people from seemingly simple acronyms has inspired audiences far and near. It is my prayer that as you read this book, you too will be empowered and inspired to live your life on purpose.

Bishop David E. Jackson, DMin

Senior Pastor

Mt. Sinai Baptist Church

Atlanta, GA

www.dejackson.org

PREFACE

Somebody say it with me, "WON'T HE DO IT!" Glory to God! I am so trying to contain myself. Anyone who knows me knows that I AM A PRAISER, so it takes me a minute to bring it down. Without telling all my business, my whole story, because it is actually supposed to be the first book. Forthcoming is "Who Am I? Abandoned but Anointed." I will extract some golden nuggets and share with you so you can feel my praise of gratitude, and ride a few of the rough roads in my journey. Let's see: Please, note the **'B.U.T'** denotes **'Better Understand This'**

* Adopted **BUT** not Aborted.

*Addicted **BUT** Delivered.

*Abused **BUT** Survived.

*Imprisoned **BUT** Set Free.

*Victim **BUT** not Vindictive.

*Lost **BUT** Found.

*Abandoned **BUT** Anointed

Yes, my GPS was badly jacked up and barely worked at all. These roads didn't all have signs on the median, and if they did, I missed them. Like the Israelites, what should have taken four years took forty but thank God for grace and mercy.

The self-will to emotions, to abusive pain, and rejection detoured me from all my childhood rearing, my private school education, my college goals and my faith to fulfill my visions and dreams. It just killed, stole and destroyed. "HIS will be done in my life." It was a set up for the mess up. BUT, there goes that acronym again. How many of you know that what God has for you it is for you? The plans HE has for you will be fulfilled and HE will get the glory. The gift God has placed inside of you does not dissipate. What will happen without the training of the gift, the stirring of the gift, or the working of the gift? It will delay the blessings manifested by the gift.

My actual gift of writing came full circle when I was 33yrs of age. In my early childhood, I thought my gift was in 'art' because I loved to draw and could color extremely well. My choice of colors blended so vividly and my ability to color within the lines was impeccable. My art designs had their own unique style and I won many art contests. I discovered this was just a phase as I soon outgrew it. It became boring and my disinterest caused me to drop it like a hot potato.

I entered into Middle school and pursued an acting career. I was still in the 'Arts' but was more interested in drama. Acting was my dream and it was at this point in my life that I was determined to be a 'Hollywood Movie Star.' Little did I know, I would keep the energetic personality and natural charisma but the Hollywood Hall of Fame was quite a ways away.

Upon getting to High school, I joined the journalism club. I enhanced my acting and moved into the next dimension of writing school plays and writing news stories for the school paper. Many began to recognize me because of my energetic personality. Although I was still acting a little here and there for the school and community, my focus was on the headliners for the news stories. I later began a 'Creative Writing' class. Oh, Yes! Creative Writing. I was in love! I wrote poem after poem and short stories as well. My poems had a different style. My short stories touched many emotions and caused energy to transpire. I won a few contests with the National Poetry Contest and my work was picked for publishing. In College, I made sure I found a creative writing class to be added on my class schedule. I also joined the Creative Writer's Guild and the Creative Writing Club. I was truly good at writing poetry and short stories. As a result, I won creative writing contests and national poetry awards. I recently stumbled across many and will share with you in an upcoming book. "With Pen in Hand" writing books and plays to one day become a movie or stage play would get me to Hollywood.

The crash and burn. Earlier I mentioned that what should've taken me four years took me forty, well it wasn't actually forty but it was longer than God had planned for me. (Jeremiah 29:11) So I am still writing, but now it's like Paul, behind the walls of prison. These are now letters to my mother, father and children. Although it was a short bid, the frequent trips for misdemeanors made it seem like a life sentence. So let me fast forward, because you have to stay anxious to get the rest of the juicy story when you purchase the book, 'Who Am I? Abandoned but Anointed." Moving on...

The prodigal daughter returns home and the new visions and dreams visit me frequently with the unction to write seasonal plays, short skits and the church newsletter @ Zion Dominion COGIC, Buffalo, NY. I eventually surrendered my position to a youth successor because my Evangelism calling was taking precedent in my life. I trained in Western NY COGIC Seminary, Project Ephesus Campus, (affiliated- CH Mason Theological Seminary) and other neighboring COGIC sister churches' training until I relocated and became a Georgia Peach. I stayed busy in the Kingdom on the streets in the Community, wherever the need; whatever the cause. I always, always, always said," I am going to write a book sharing my life story. It was not by coincidence that every leader God placed in my life to teach me or be my spiritual covering or under which I was placed to be a servant for God in the ministry was an AUTHOR. A shout out to my current core leaders; Bishop Dr. David E Jackson (dejackson.org)- "Work Your Room"; Apostle Gloria Holden(gloriaholden.com) - "Wounded Soul" (this book really ministered to my spirit) and so many more. My Presbyter Colleagues, and spiritual daughters are Authors and my life was created by the GREATEST author, God the Father – The Bible.

Delayed but Not Denied! Yes, May 13th @ 7am, the Holy Spirit spoke clearly with new instructions not to go to my normal hair salon of ten years but to go to another salon and get braids. This request really didn't seem unusual to me, because it was a desire I had down in my ShaNaNa, since returning from an amazing empowering mission trip in Ghana, Accra. Ghana is still very much alive in my Spirit and on my mind. So, I called my tax client who is a professional hairstylist to get my Ghana look. She of course was fully booked but she called her colleague, who was available. I had connected with the Hook Up!

I met Ms. Diamond Mock, who is an Author of ("Just Stand", "Embracing Single & Saved" and many more) at Embellish Salon, in

Douglasville, GA. It was indeed a divine connection because I also met Prophetess Odessia Brewer (salon owner and operator) her sons: Zion, Xavier Brewer; Apostle Dr. Gwenn Washington, and Sister Glenda Kelsey. Apostle Dr. Gwenn & I were sharing about the Praise and Worship and Character of Courtesy and Power of Love that you feel when you go to Africa, as she was going back to Kenya or Nairobi. I could definitely relate because I had just returned from Ghana, Accra. I tell you the Spirit was so High and Alive in that Salon from just sharing the experience. Why then did Prophetess Odessia Brewer ask us to pray It happened just like this thereafter. The gathering of the Circle (prayer & prophetic); The Breaking of Yokes & Strongholds (tears, speaking of tongues, confession); The Holy Spirit Speaks to Me (It's T.I.M.E- trust in me entirely); The Relationship & The Hook Up (Diamond provides the resources for the Editor, Graphic Designer & Publisher); The Echo (It's T.I.M.E-trust in me entirely); The Delivery of the Birth of the Vision.

I hope you enjoy the book, Acronym Preacher. I begin the first chapter with the first evidence of the Nataph in the acronym gift, which is my original first seven-minute sermon, in Homiletics class in 1999 at Zion Dominion COGIC before the great Bishop GE Patterson, Superintendent Jeffrey Carter, Evangelist Rodriquez Spencer; Bishop Roderick Hennings. The evidence of working your gift and training in your calling is imperative, and this you will witness after the first chapter. Discover the impossibilities with your gift and experience God's promises as they prevail.

I leave you with these (3) thoughts: Your gift is a divine present from God that will last forever, just work it! Follow the Holy Spirit in everything you do! Divine connections are blessings to your life.

TABLE OF CONTENTS

Chapter 1: Scripture   Ecclesiastes 3:1-8 (KJV)

3 To everything there is a season, and a time to every purpose under the heaven:

2 A time to be born, and a time to die; a time to plant, and a time to pluck up that which is planted;

3 A time to kill, and a time to heal; a time to break down, and a time to build up;

4 A time to weep, and a time to laugh; a time to mourn, and a time to dance;

5 A time to cast away stones, and a time to gather stones together; a time to embrace, and a time to refrain from embracing;

6 A time to get, and a time to lose; a time to keep, and a time to cast away;

7 A time to rend, and a time to sew; a time to keep silence, and a time to speak;

8 A time to love, and a time to hate; a time of war, and a time of peace.

[9] What profit hath he that worketh in that wherein he laboureth?

[10] I have seen the travail, which God hath given to the sons of men to be exercised in it.

[11] He hath made everything beautiful in his time: also he hath set the world in their heart, so that no man can find out the work that God maketh from the beginning to the end.

[12] I know that there is no good in them, but for a man to rejoice, and to do good in his life.

[13] And also that every man should eat and drink, and enjoy the good of all his labour, it is the gift of God.

¹⁴ I know that, whatsoever God doeth, it shall be forever: nothing can be put to it, nor any thing taken from it: and God doeth it, that men should fear before him.

¹⁵ That which hath been is now; and that which is to be hath already been; and God requireth that which is past.

¹⁶ And moreover I saw under the sun the place of judgment, that wickedness was there; and the place of righteousness, that iniquity was there.

¹⁷ I said in mine heart, God shall judge the righteous and the wicked: for there is a time there for every purpose and for every work.

¹⁸ I said in mine heart concerning the estate of the sons of men that God might manifest them, and that they might see that they themselves are beasts.

¹⁹ For that which befalleth the sons of men befalleth beasts; even one thing befalleth them: as the one dieth, so dieth the other; yea, they have all one breath; so that a man hath no preeminence above a beast: for all is vanity.

²⁰ All go unto one place; all are of the dust, and all turn to dust again.

²¹ Who knoweth the spirit of man that goeth upward, and the spirit of the beast that goeth downward to the earth?

²² Wherefore I perceive that there is nothing better, than that a man should rejoice in his own works; for that is his portion: for who shall bring him to see what shall be after him?

Chapter 1: Do You Know What T.I.M.E It Is?

So here we are the very first sign of my acronym gift. This was also my first seven-minute oration before my Pastor, the Superintendent of COGIC Seminary, the Bishop, Leader of COGIC-WNY District 1, Evangelists, Professors, Chancellors, Visiting Pastors of my colleague's churches, my church family, my family, friends and major spectators. If I haven't painted a vivid picture, the church is overflowed (1000 seats) and I am definitely nervous. My two semesters in homiletic studies was about to be critiqued, evaluated, questioned and commended by all these generals and senior Ambassadors for Christ within 7 minutes.

I can remember very distinctly when the Holy Spirit spoke (Nataph) to me on that bright and early Saturday morning. He gave me the acronym for T.I.M.E which would be a part of the title and even added the blue print to put my outline together for the message. We had no specific style/format to follow for the sermon, but it had to include (3) of the (9) types of sermons. My top three were: expository, hortatory, and evangelistic. I was pretty confident of how the Nataph (Holy Spirit) was downloading info to me, until this day! Needless to say, I did very well, although I didn't use all the points in my outline. I "brought it" as they say, with energy, truth and life. Listening to Bishop Patterson, Bishop Blake and Bishop Ford throughout my 15-year tenure as COGIC denomination definitely marked my method.

So as you read this first chapter, it's actually an assignment with valuable information inspired by the Holy Spirit, that I didn't know how to compose, because I was in training of my calling with a gift; Acronym Preaching. Out of this whole message, it's the subject that's the highlight. As you read the rest of the book, you will see how God develops and grows this gift. How He uses my life experiences, middle of the night prayer watches, grocery store experiences, vacations and even confrontations to perfect His purpose to speak to the body of Christ and be a witness for the Kingdom of God.

My name is Evangelist Cindy Betts and my title today is: "Do You Know What Time It Is?

The subject is: Time Management in Transition (Spiritually ready; put aside deeds of darkness)

The meaning for the word time is different from the normal word. The Holy Spirit actually defined it to be:

T-Transform   I-Iniquities   M-Magnify   E-Eternity

My Proposition is transforming worldly time into spiritual time. So I ask you the question, "How much time are you investing in your eternity with God?"

Let's examine the word Transform in its biblical Definition.

Romans 12:2 "Do not conform any longer to the pattern of this world, but be transformed by the renewing of your mind, then you will be able to test and approve what God's will is... HIS good and pleasing and perfect will."

This is denoting a change, a sacrifice. Greater is he that is in you, than He that is of the world.

In the book of Ecclesiastes 3: 1-15, every interest of human life has its proper time and its opposite has its own time, whether in life it's physical, economic, social or political. But what does man gain? God made man busy with this and that and those fine things in its time. Tests of pleasure, status and intellectual pursuits none of which are sufficient to give meaning to life (Seek Ye First the Kingdom Of God.)

What I mean brothers and sisters is time is short. (I Cor 7:29-) All the worldly are hastened to the end. Life in this world shouldn't be our utmost concern. Our greatest attention should be directed toward eternity (heavenly home) On the other hand, God put eternity in Man's mind without which man cannot grasp his purpose throughout time.

Spiritual is more complex. It never dies. It supersedes the flesh regardless of the time. It requires Kingdom understanding. "No Worry to Time." We must receive eternal life before we can share in it together with others.

Eternal life is to know God the Father and Jesus Christ and be in a personal and intimate relationship with Him.

Entering into a meaningful relationship with God is not living in the world where "Self" is the only true subject and other things are objects. The world is not just a place where whatever will happen, will happen or whatever is meant to be will be. We are not just going through the motions of living we are participants in God's plan.

Realize time is in God's hand and if we are in HIS presence, there is "No Worry to Time." I ask the question, "What time do you have?"

Verses 16-22 in chapter three of Ecclesiastes shows faith and belief that judgement is coming. If wickedness fills the place of justice, then God who takes account of time must judge the just and the wicked.

Life 'Under the Sun' is seen through the eyes of the unredeemed. It's characterized by iniquities, uncertainties, unpredictable changes in fortune and violations of justice.

Life 'Above the Sun' is seen through the eyes of God.

Let's view the two Greek variances of the word Time as it is defined to be 'Season'.

Kairos in the Greek means: (quality) primarily due measures; due proportion, signified 'a fixed or definite period as in Season'. (Romans 5:6)

Chronos in the Greek means: (quantity) space of time (long or short) implies duration. (I Thessalonians 5:1) The seasons are the period before and after the Parousia.

There is a reason for the season. Season's purpose is to produce. Timing is everything. Plant a seed, you nurture it. God has perfect timing for our lives, yet it is so easy to be impatient which leads to disaster.

So, after all that has been said, what is my point about T.I.M.E.?

Jesus never cared about time. HE was the first being to be destroyed by death and HE brought life and immorality to light. Don't wait to have to give an account to God for a wasted life. Build your relationship with God now.

Time to pray not curse.

Time to get to know Him, not for what He has done, but who He is.

Time to make that change, like the man in the mirror.

Time to create a plan for eternity not destruction.

Time to fill one's self with God's word (audio, visual, literature, fellowship, etc.) not drugs or alcohol.

Time to let God bring an end to emotional and fleshly attachments.

Time to be comforted and counseled with God's love, not prostitution or fornication.

"In the time of my favor, I heard you and in the day of salvation, I helped you."

(II Corinthians 6:2)

I tell you, now is the time of God's favor. Now is the day of salvation.

Chapter 2: Scripture Matthew 11: 11-15 (NKJV)

11 "Assuredly, I say to you, among those born of women there has not risen one greater than John the Baptist; but he who is least in the kingdom of heaven is greater than he. 12 And from the days of John the Baptist until now the kingdom of heaven suffers violence, and the violent take it by force. 13 For all the prophets and the law prophesied until John. 14 And if you are willing to receive *it,* he is Elijah who is to come. 15 He who has ears to hear, let him hear!"

Chapter 2: What's Your A.L.I.B.I.?

We are definitely living in the last days; 'Signs of the Times', wouldn't you agree? In the Greek, it's called the 'Parousia' meaning the 2nd Coming. As I check out the latest news incidents, and the twentieth century version of (II Timothy 3:1-5 NKJV.), it is apparent that the last days are upon us. In case you don't know those verses by heart, go ahead and read it here for yourself.

3 But know this, that in the last days perilous times will come: 2 For men will be lovers of themselves, lovers of money, boasters, proud, blasphemers, disobedient to parents, unthankful, unholy, 3 unloving, unforgiving, slanderers, without self-control, brutal, despisers of good, 4 traitors, headstrong, haughty, lovers of pleasure rather than lovers of God, 5 having a form of godliness but denying its power. And from such people turn away!

There is no diggity, no doubt, the enemy is running rampant, but it's all a part of his tricks to get us distracted and decoyed from our vision and more important our purpose to fulfill the kingdom of God. When you are focused on your purpose, you overcome your struggles and are effective in the kingdom of God. When we are not, we are then denying Christ like Judas, because we are not operating in our gift. We are not moving in our Anointing and living life according to the principles of God as instructed by the B.I.B.L.E. (basic instructions before leaving the earth).

Our navigation system is being rerouted from the destination; therefore we are not fulfilling our purpose with faith for the kingdom of God. The detour leads us down a road of procrastination. We then become 'T. A. C.' Members (talk about it Christians) in the body of Christ. A T.A.C member's conversation is full of A.L.I.B.I.'S and sounds like...

Oh, God gave me a vision and I am going to start when... I know what God can do; I am just waiting on... I would've had it or done it a long time ago, but... It is so easy to be spiritually distracted. What's so ironic is we confess that we know Jesus.

We profess our love for him and we even praise him like we have lost our minds, but slip and fall fast and hard for the diversion to lose focus on our purpose for the kingdom of God. The enemy laughs and has even convinced you to denounce or diffuse your faith.

What I need to know is where are the 'B.A.C.' Members (be about it Christians)? They are the producers of fruit, because they are connected to the vine of the Father! So, now I am asking you, 'What's Your A.L.I.B.I? Webster and Meriam dictionary defines the word alibi as:

1. Law. The defense by an accused person of having been elsewhere at the time an alleged offense was committed.
2. An excuse, especially to avoid blame.
3. A person used as one's excuse: My sick grandmother was my alibi for missing school.

But let me share with you in detail the spiritual meaning of A.L.I.B.I.

A- Abound: be plentiful, be abundant, be numerous, proliferate, overflow with, team with, be packed with, be crowded with, be thronged with, and be alive with.

Wow, there is never lack in any area when we are about our Father's business; when we are maturing and training in our gifts; when we are studying, and working in the kingdom with a heart for God. Having motives of passion, faith and righteousness, the people of God cannot be hallway Christians. We cannot go just far enough and then quit! Nor can we do things just for self. It must always be for the glory of God. When you take control of your flesh; pray His purpose for your life; stay focused and operate in God's will, you will live in abundance.

The bible says, "The thief cometh not, but for to steal, and to kill, and to destroy; I am come that they might have life, and that they might have *it* more abundantly. (John10:10 NKLV)

We believers have to be on top of the game because the enemy has more game than a human mind could even imagine, let alone endure. So we need to turn it up to 150.

Come on somebody and praise God with me! Just standing on God's word with a mustard seed of faith, in the one who came to give us life more abundantly gives us victory over any game the enemy sets up to play in the battle field of our mind.

(II Corinthians 9:8 AMP)

And God is able to make all grace (every favor and earthly blessing) come to you in abundance, so that you may always and under all circumstances and whatever the need be self-sufficient (possessing enough to require no aid or support and furnished in abundance for every good work and charitable donation.

L- Listen: to pay attention to someone or something in order to hear what is being said, sung, played etc.

The Holy Spirit will speak clearly to You! (Psalm 37:23 KJV) "The steps of a good man are ordered by the LORD: and he delighteth in his way. LORD in all caps is pronounced *LAWD- Hebrew meaning Jehovah, the great I AM. Our LORD has a purpose in you and the enemy is after it. When you are focused on your purpose, you overcome your struggles and are effective in the kingdom of God. It is so important to know the voice of God and to be led by the Holy Spirit. Why do we listen to the Holy Spirit? Well, there are many functions of the Holy Spirit and how He does a good work in you. Let's examine a few.

- I Corinthians 12:7-11—He distributes spiritual gifts according to His will.
- John 14:16 – He comforts us.
- John 14: 26 – He teaches us.
- Ephesians 1:13; 4:30—He remains as a seal of promise upon our hearts until the day of Jesus' return.
- Luke 12:12; I Corinthians 2:6-10—He guides and is a counselor, leading us in the way we should go as He reveals God's truth.

So, have you ever wondered if it was you speaking or the Holy Spirit? This is how you can discern between your own thoughts and the Holy Spirit leading. A key way of discerning is vivid. The spirit does not speak with audible words. No not one.

Rather, He guides us through an inner voice (see John 16:13) and our own consciences (see Romans 9:1), and a few other quiet subtle ways. Key word is 'quiet'. The number one and most important way to recognize the Holy Spirit's guidance is to be familiar with the Word of God. (Ephesians 6:17). The Word is the "sword of the spirit" and according to (John 16: 12-14); the spirit speaks to us through it and He reveals the will of God for our lives. He will also bring specific scriptures to mind at times when we need them most (John 14:26) Thank You Holy Spirit!

Knowledge of the word of God helps us to discern whether or not our desires come from the Holy Spirit. We must test (try the spirit by the spirit) our inner voice against Scripture. One thing is for sure and that is the Holy Spirit will never prod us to do anything contrary to God's Word. If it conflicts and goes against the Bible, then it is not from the Holy Spirit, so don't do it! Don't listen to that voice, disregard it totally. We are so blessed to be the only living creatures able to communicate with the Father with the help of the Holy Spirit. (I Thessalonians 5:17); continual prayer with the Father will keep our hearts and minds open to the Holy Spirits leading, but it also allows the spirit to speak on our behalf: "In the same way the Spirit helps us in our weakness, the spirit himself intercedes for us (Romans 8:26-27; and he who searches our hearts knows the mind of the spirit because the spirit intercedes for the saints in accordance with God's will.

Evidence of the spirit is His fruit in our lives (Galatians 5:22). Walking in the spirit, we will continue to see these qualities grow and mature in us, and they will become evident to others as well. Here is a BIG Warning, warning. Danger, Danger! We have the choice whether or not to accept the Holy Spirit's guidance. When we know the will of God, but do not follow it, we are setting ourselves up for the mess up. (Acts 7:51 & I Thessalonians 5:19.) Resisting the spirit's work in our lives and pursuing the desire to follow your own way grieves Him (Ephesians 4:30).

We should NEVER grieve the Holy Spirit!

I – Interact: act in such a way as to have an effect on another; be in contact; have dealings; work together.

Please close your circle and be with like-minded, like- spirited people. People that want more of GOD and are living to discover how to be more like Christ; people wanting to know how to reap the harvest from the tree of life; people enjoying the plans predestined with blessings in their lives; people seeking a deeper anointing and knowledge of their calling; people willing to work on their inner issues and trust God and believe in the promises to be delivered, healed and set free; people seeking wisdom and discernment to give a real prophetic word with a distinct revelation and quick manifestation.

Check out (Hebrews 10:25 AMP) Not forsaking or neglecting to assemble together (as believers), as is the habit of some people, but admonishing (warning, urging, and encouraging) one another, and all the more faithfully as you see the day approaching.

I Love this cliché'; 'Make your haters your motivators.' The Father made it known many times to us that He would make our enemy our footstool. Don't believe me; read Luke 20:42-43; Psalm 110:1; Acts 2:34-35; Matthew 22:44; Acts 2:35 or Mark 12:36.

You have haters because, "we are peculiar (standing apart from other people- belonging distinctively or especially to 1 person, group or kind) the God's Property People. You have haters because you are effective in the kingdom. You have haters because you are true to your calling. You refuse to 'play church' or 'run for positions.' You have haters because you won't sway, barter or swap your faith for religion, tradition or theology.

Every new level doesn't have new devils (don't give the enemy no credit or space in your territory), but new challenges and oppositions to your faith. Get a made-up heart and mind to live out your destiny and your purpose in this life for the glory of God and his kingdom. I want to make one thing clear.

Don't act like you're better than anyone who may be your hater, because they have issues just like you and me, but losing sleep and energy focusing on the wrong things or the wrong person. That is why it's so important   to be real with yourself and God in every area of your life. If you don't know your gift or your purpose, ask God to reveal it to you. If you don't have your own vision, support your brother or sister's. You most definitely should be supporting your church leader!

B- Believe: accept (something) as true; feel sure of the truth.

It is written that faith without works is dead! (James 2:26.) If you don't know by now, having under gone any of life's ordeals, we serve a benignant God. The lineage and covenant with Him since our Father Abraham, and renewed by the blood of Jesus Christ brings blessings, grace, favor, mercy and strategy.

Now just allow yourself to flash back real quickly with me. Real talk, some of us are sitting here today still living in the past. Let that mess go! Let it Go and Free yourself! Free somebody else. Forgive, forget and Let God do what he needs to do to bless You! Move out of God's way and grab a hold of the life that He has intended for you to enjoy while you are living on this earth. How? You know, by walking in your purpose, birthing your vision, working your gifts. Come on, now. Reality check. Just look at all the people, places and things you have invested in, sacrificed for and imparted immeasurable trust into, but in return have been rejected, forgotten or avoided. All God wants and asks is for us to trust Him with the faith of a mustard seed. Amazing analogy: if you have ever taken a straight pin (this is the best object to take hold of it) and split the seed open, there are thousands of seeds within that pin head size mustard seed. Let's face it, God trusts us to give just ten percent (that belongs to Him) of our income as our tithes (to be considered a seed in our heavenly account) and we keep the ninety. Just an FYI, it's the offerings that you can count on as your harvest seed when you need to make a heavenly withdrawal. It's amazing how we have such a hard time with trusting God with what's already His.

I mean we get bent all out of shape. The funny part of this is Uncle Sam doesn't even give you an option of trust; they take theirs off the top and will even come look for you if you are dead and gone.

What's also mind blowing (I have done it myself) is that I can't get ahead, or past broke or not enough mentality. A bill is there at my door before I even get a check, and has absorbed all the money I have from the check I just received. I wouldn't trust God even when he screamed 'Try Me' and see in Malachi, but instead I sang the woe is me song on repeat without breaking a sweat. I stayed stuck seated in the "oh God, where are you?' section of the Woe is me concert. We are so fast to sell out and deny our faith and therefore deny our Father, feeling totally convinced that it's impossible to survive the storm, or be blessed or fulfill the vision that God birthed in us! REPEAT after me, EMOTION without DEVOTION causes COMMOTION!

I-Immutability: Unable to be changed

Once you get here… STAND! You have a non-changing mind and attitude to be the best King's Kid ever to inherit the throne. Understand that the Father is the same God yesterday, today and tomorrow. He never changes. Our Father reminds us in His word (Romans 2:11) and if that's not sufficient (Acts 10:34)," God is no respecter of persons as God shows no partiality. So please don't flip the script on God or behave in a bipolar disposition.

God the Father has over 4,000 promises that He is waiting to fulfill to every HEIR of the THRONE. Understand who you are TO God and Who you are IN God. Then make Him your everything in life. Do not sell your birth right to Satan. Do not let his angels trick you into denying your inheritance and demise your royalty. Do not let the enemy disconnect you from your source of dunamis power. Do not let the enemy come and steal, kill and destroy You in your health, finances and relationships. Do not be robbed of your vision, depleted of your purpose and left out from receiving your crown. Don't give up your joy, let alone surrender it.

Do boldly as I beseech each and every one of you, take it all back by force! Be effective in the kingdom for the glory of God! Be a victorious warrior in the army of the Lord.

How strong is your A.L.I.B.I.? Enjoy these encouraging alibis from great people you may know.

- "It's all right letting yourself go, as long as you can get yourself back." Mick Jagger
- "Do not bite at the bait of pleasure till you know there is no hook beneath it." Thomas Jefferson
- "About the only time losing is more fun than winning is when you're fighting temptation."
- "Serving one's own passions is the greatest slavery." Thomas Fuller
- "I am, indeed a king, because I know how to rule myself." Pietro Aretino, 1537
- "You have to decide what your highest priorities are and have the courage, pleasantly, smilingly, unapologetically to say 'no' to other things. And the way to do that is by having a bigger 'yes' burning inside. The enemy of the 'best' is often the 'good'. Stephen Covey

Chapter 3: Scripture Psalm 91 (AMP)

He, who dwells in the shelter of the Most High, will remain secure *and* rest in the shadow of the Almighty [whose power no enemy can withstand].

[2] I will say of the LORD, "He is my refuge and my fortress, My God, in whom I trust [with great confidence, and on whom I rely]!" [3] For He will save you from the trap of the fowler, And from the deadly pestilence.

[4] He will cover you *and* completely protect you with His pinions, and under His wings you will find refuge; His faithfulness is a shield and a wall. [5] You will not be afraid of the terror of night, nor of the arrow that flies by day,

[6] nor of the pestilence that stalks in darkness, nor of the destruction (sudden death) that lays waste at noon. [7] A thousand may fall at your side, and ten thousand at your right hand,
but danger will not come near you.

[8] You will only [be a spectator as you] look on with your eyes, and witness the [divine] repayment of the wicked [as you watch safely from the shelter of the Most High].

[9] Because you have made the LORD, [who is] my refuge, Even the Most High, your dwelling place, [10] No evil will befall you, Nor will any plague come near your tent. [11] For He will command His angels in regard to you, To protect *and* defend *and* guard you in all your ways [of obedience and service]. [12] They will lift you up in their hands, So that you do not [even] strike your foot against a stone. [13] You will tread upon the lion and cobra; The young lion and the serpent you will trample underfoot. [14] "Because he set his love on Me, therefore I will save him; I will set him [securely] on high, because he knows My name [he confidently trusts and relies on Me, knowing I will never abandon him, no, never]. [15] "He will call upon Me, and I will answer him; I will be with him in trouble; I will rescue him and honor him. [16] "With a long life I will satisfy him, And I will let him see My salvation."

Chapter 3: It's In The D.N.A.

It's not just what you know, but who you know. I know everyone has heard that saying before, and depending on the situation, it holds a hundred percent true. Let me just give you a bit of biblical background before we get deep into this chapter. The psalm- Hebrew word "Tehillim" means "praises". The theme of psalm is prayer and praise, because the psalm was written to be either a song or a prayer. There are 150 psalms organized into five (5) books. Psalm 150 is the last book and also known as the doxology (expression of praise to God) for the entire psalter.

The Baptist often sing this doxology in their morning worship service as the responsive hymn. There are many writers of Psalm, to name a few: David, Sons of Korah (musically gifted family) Asaph (a musically and prophetic gifted Levite), Moses, Solomon, Heman, Ethan and the priests and Levites with musical gifts & responsibilities in sacred worship during David's reign. Each psalm was classified in a category: praise, thanksgiving, prayer, liturgical, etc.

Psalm 91 is a song of trust and protection. It was determined to have been written by Moses during the journey through the wilderness, shortly after the plague of the fiery serpents; when the children of Israel, having returned to a better spirit, where they again received the favor of Jehovah (Numbers 21:6). We are about to go in, so tell your brother or sister; It's in the D.N.A. It's not just what you know, but who you know.

As I mentioned in the beginning of the book, my spiritual hermeneutics comes to me in acronyms, thus where the title was derived 'acronym preacher.' So although the old cliché; 'it's not just what you know but who you know' is ancient it still has major vitality today. I am here to tell you, you need both, the what and the who. Here are three (3) reasons:

1. The **what** positions you for the **who** to work on your behalf.

2. The **what** also gives you access or leverage to the **who**.

3. The **what** is your confidence, trust bka faith. It's the faith that motivates the **who** (God) for His favor, healing and protection.

Some of us need to stir up the what-Faith because we are sitting at the pity party in the woe is me section, when you should be in the down with o.p.p. section (operating in praise and prayer) Are you blaming the blessing (job, car, new relationship, money) for missing service, bible study, and spending time with God? Yes, just too busy (belonging under satan's yoke) as some folks would say, with distractions. If you can't handle the blessings in the prosperity season, what are you going to do when there is a famine? Now is the time to turn up your S.W.A.G. (Serving. Worship. Accountability. Giving).

Could it be that you're just trapped in the battle field of your mind, that you are cursed? Or maybe brainwashed because at some point in your life (like me) you were told you're of no worth, value or purpose. This is often referred to as a generational curse. Well I know generational curses are a lie, because I'm adopted and don't know any traces of my ancestry. So I come to give Satan notice right now in the almighty name of Jesus that the enemy has no power over the most high God that we serve. The Blood of Jesus paid it all and we all are redeemed! Who the Son set free is free in deed. Hallelujah… Go ahead and shout in a strong praise and Shabach the Lord, wherever you are! Break down those walls of curses like Jericho. Let me help somebody today. The only generational curse written in the bible is the fall of man in Genesis 3:14-19. And because God is so sovereign, he gives us generational blessings through Abram in Genesis 12: 2-3. So let's not get it twisted! The Devil is and always will be a liar! Go get your blessings!

So I asked the Holy Spirit, How do we break the chains? How do we receive this V.I.P (Victory Interceding Persistently) protection against the wiles of the enemy? How does the weapons work that form against us, not prosper? He spoke and said, "It's in the D.N.A.! The D.N.A.? Yes, the D.N.A. Okay, so does anyone watch any of those crime investigative shows i.e. Bones, Trace or CSI? Okay, well what about baby mama drama like Maury Povich or Dr. Phil and they have to take the DNA test to determine paternity? The DNA is the hereditary material in humans and almost all other organisms.

DNA proves without a shadow of a doubt, who the parent is (the hereditary relationship). So if I may, allow me to hurry up and take my time and break down the Spiritual D.N.A.

D- Discover God at another level:

Get into an intimate relationship with God. Learn and know the love of God in Christ Jesus. Get into a place of nearness and divine familiarity. Seek to dwell in God's presence. Stay in His face and connect with Him.

When I first met my husband, I built a desire to go to another level with this man. The more time we spent together, the more I learned. The more we shared, the more I fell in love with Him. Not only do I trust him, I have faith that he will protect me because of our love, our deep relationship. All that we have and will endure together is because of the invested time we spend with one another. I trust my leader Bishop Dr. David E Jackson, because I know he is not only a wise man of God, but he is the 'POPO- APD's finest (Atlanta Police Department) and packing with a Gloc9! So I feel secure and have peace, when I'm in his presence.

The blessings promised in Psalm 91: verses 1-8 are not for all believers, but for those who live in close fellowship with God. It's a consistency. You see, there's a condition with a promise.

Read: 'He who dwells… (condition) Shall rest… (promise). 'If you say of the Lord… (condition) he shall… (promise). Look at the different aspects of this protection based on the condition of the promise.

"Most High"- Greater than any threat we face and "Shaddai"- All sufficient. He says, we can remain secure and rest in the 'shadow' of the almighty. So I looked up the word shadow. Wow, listen to this definition. 'To follow (a person) about secretly, in order to keep watch over his movements. Great nearness. Constant presence of God.' This right here blew my mind. God's constant presence. Divine stalking! Divine secret service. But wait, then I looked up the word Almighty. Check this out. It means having the power to confront & destroy your enemy.

I can shout right now, "If God be for me, I don't care who's against me!" I know deep in my spirit the weapons will not prosper, I don't care how they form! Praise El Shaddai. Let's look at verse three. [3] For He will save you from the trap of the fowler, And from the deadly pestilence. It is here that Moses tells in detail as to what happens when you enter into the Holy of Holies… Your secret place… to the What (trust/faith) that connects with the Who (God) and the omnipotent power is then manifested.

N –Never Forget Who God Is!

Do you know 'Who' the Father is, that is your daddy and my daddy? Big Papa! In verses nine & ten it reads, just to remind you: [9] Because you have made the LORD, [who is] my refuge, Even the Most High, your dwelling place,[10] No evil will befall you, Nor will any plague come near your tent.

Sweet Jesus! My God, My God! If you Say and you make (condition); then No evil, No disaster (promise). I am not sure how you are feeling right now, but I am feeling like Royalty. A truly spoiled king's kid. I ingested this psalm in my mind, body and soul. Everything revolves **around OUR SHADDAI.** Everything operates in accordance with the conditions and laws that HE has set. Everything is within His plan and will work within His realm and not a minute or day before or after. The nature revolves around Him and His control. The nations and the lives of all humanity revolve around the LORD. This is plainly stated in Psalm 33 starting at verse 6 and ending at verse 19. So DON'T go before GOD. Stay within His will and enjoy the plans He has for your life, because there is no plan or scheme that can stand up against God's. Ultimately, it is the Lord's plan that will stand forever and His intentions can never be shaken.

This leads me to something the disciple Peter wrote in I Peter 5: 6-7. Peter was writing this letter to the believers scattered throughout Asia Minor, which is modern day Turkey. Peter was encouraging them to submit to God and resist the devil in a world that increasingly opposes believers and the biblical truths they uphold.

6 "Humble yourselves, therefore, under God's mighty hand, that he may lift you up in due time. 7 Cast all your anxiety on Him because He cares for you.

The operative word in the instructions is 'humble.' I read on the PsyBlog under a study done by psychologist Pelin Kesebir in 2014; that "Humility involves a willingness to accept the self's limits and its place in the grand scheme of things, accompanied by the low levels of self-preoccupation." He referred to humility as 'a quiet ego' and demonstrated the variety of different ways of how surprisingly powerful it can be. Humility soothes the soul, invokes excellent leadership, higher self-control, better work performance, higher grades, less prejudice and better relationships, just to name a few. After reading all this, I really know why the enemy loves to keep us carnal, disobedient and not under submission to authority. The Devil is LIAR!

I often think when I would watch the President of the United States of America, or Foreign Diplomats that have all the Top Security, walking on foot, motorcades and even in the aircrafts, how powerful and secure they must feel. Well, they can't touch our Almighty God. I came to realize reading verses 11 -13 of Psalm 91, that we have the top of the line and finest security in all the world! We have daily divine angelic forces from the most high's army 24/7. The Greek word for Angel is 'Angelos' and it means messenger. They are God's heavenly messengers or servants (read more in Hebrews 1: 13-14) that are delegated by God himself, to be on the fore front of our battles as we be about our Father's business. My God, my God! We truly have to do NOTHING when all hell (havoc) breaks loose, but just have a talk with our Father(prayer) then conclude in a high praise, because our angels are already on it! One thing about the battle, it belongs to the Lord so Victory is Ours! Does anyone else have a helium head and peacock strut right about now, besides me? These angels are commissioned to protect, defend and guard you in all your ways, without you or me lifting a finger. Ask your enemy, situation, condition, whatever it is, DO YOU KNOW WHO & WHOSE I AM? So NOW, You must…

A- Activate Your Faith!

In The Name (The Who). Prayer is the practice of the presence of God. When we pray, we pray in the name of Jesus.

In the Bible era, a person's name described his character. A person's name tells you who the person is and what you can expect from him. Let's refer back to the psalm where it denotes the names; shadow of the most high, fortress, refugee and almighty. We are to use the NAME as weapons in prayer warfare. We use the NAME of the Lord Jesus the same way as you would use the promises of God in scripture. Do you pray God's promises back to HIM? There are over 4,000 promises. I beseech you to get this little book called, "God's Promises for Your Every Need" by Thomas Nelson.

To pray in Jesus name is to pray for His sake; to use his name as your reference; to claim Calvary's victory for your need; to acknowledge his full role as God's anointed; to pray with all His authority.

To pray in Jesus Name is the key to ALL power and promises of God. Jesus explicitly instructs us that we should pray in His name. Read with me below, John 14:13-14.

13And I will do whatever you ask, ask in my name, so that the Son may bring glory to the Father. You may ask me for anything in my name and I will do it." Or if that wasn't etched out clearly enough, how about John 15:16 "You didn't choose me, but I chose you to go and bear fruit, fruit that will last. Then the Father will give you whatever you ask in my name. Last but not least, John 16: 23-24: "I tell you the truth, my Father will give you whatever you ask in my name. Until now you have not asked for anything in my name. Ask and you will receive, and your joy will be complete.

Done deal. That settles it. The ink doesn't get any plainer or dryer than this. Sealed and notarized by Jesus Christ the Son of the Almighty God we serve, Himself.

God the Father is so sovereign and knows that life deals us a bad hand in different areas of our lives and at different seasons, that He and His son Jesus have over 900 names in the bible (See Christiananswers.net). They want us to be fully equipped with armor in our tool belt, and have whatever weapon we need to speak into the atmosphere and bring down the warfare.

God the Father and His son Jesus wants us to use whatever you need for them to be for you and to be to you in your daily prayers and daily conversations. There is power alone in the name of Jesus! It's ALL in the D.N.A!

Chapter 4: Scripture   John 10:10 (AMP)

John 10:10 (AMP) will be our focus scripture and verse. 10" The thief comes only in order to steal and kill and destroy. I came that they may have and enjoy life and have it in abundance (to the fullest, till it overflows.

Chapter 4: Do You Have An A.D.T. System?

Jesus had one main purpose; that being the salvation of the sheep. This is described as free access to pasture and fullness of life. The benefit of being under His protection because He fulfilled his purpose on Calvary and by His gift allows us (sheep) to experience the best life can offer. In this scripture verse, John's emphasis on eternal life takes on a new significance. Here Jesus Christ gives a whole new meaning to living by providing full satisfaction and perfect guidance. I immediately reflect to the 23rd psalm. Just like children know the voice of their earthly parents, we too must know the voice of our spiritual Father. The only way to the Father is through the Son, our Lord and Savior Jesus Christ.

The thought of locking up my prize possessions and even having an A.D.T. alarm system, puts me literally on alert. It even made me tear up a few ninja warfare suits. When I retrospect over my life and visually see the ambience and era that I was raised up in, I can truly identify more with this scripture and the fact that we are living in the era of the last days. I grew up in my early adolescents in the Spring Garden projects of North Philadelphia, Pa. Even back then, we could keep our back doors unlocked and the windows cracked at night. No one had an alarm system or knew what a low jack was on cars. Our cell phones were huge, but user friendly. The computers had the limited required phish ware if any. Stop it! I already hear you thinking, how old is she? Lol. No Ma'am, no Sir I am still young at heart. I believe phishing didn't come out until the late 80's and then successfully attempted until the mid-90's and it was in that era, the software was later developed. So there you have it.

Back to my point, today we have alarm systems that come with sensors & laser beams. We have passcodes, touch ID and tracking devices on cell phones, major phish ware, and spy ware and windows defenders on computers. The security systems are so high tech now you can watch your homes and your kids on your phones. The cars have built in cameras on mirrors in the bumpers all around. Purses have double straps and chains.

Animals have chips. The enemy is hard at it using any and all tactics to steal our salvation and separate us from the love of Christ and sound doctrine with sin.

There are false teachers, wolves dressed in sheep clothing, and the father of lies has set up a camp everywhere to lead us, the sheep astray. Set up traps to deceive our hearts, poison our minds and corrupt our souls. So like pest control, we need to use strong preventive maintenance. We need to install and activate the top of the line security alert system. We need our A.D.T. system on at all times. Now just in case someone is reading this and thinks I am promoting ADT security systems, I am NOT. But I am encouraging and promoting your already installed, perfectly created, divinely planned A.D.T system. My purpose is to give you some detail on the instructions on how to work the alarm system.

A- Access Codes

You must change yours frequently. Unlike some programs and merchants that send you an email to change your password every sixty or ninety days, this doesn't happen with this type of A.D.T. system.

You do however have the Holy Spirit as your technical support and through discernment, will signal you when it's time to change your access codes. You will get an A.D.T. alert to STOP telling everybody what you are going through and just go through it. Or you will be signaled to cry out and just tell Jesus, who has already undergone the blemish of this trial and made the way for you to come out of it. So I came across this scripture in 1 Corinthians 10:13 in the Amplified. Read this with me out loud, please.

13 "No temptation(regardless of its source) has overtaken or enticed you that is not common to human experience (nor is any temptation unusual or beyond human resistance); but God is faithful (to his word- He is compassionate and trustworthy), and He will not let you be tempted beyond your ability to (resist) but along with the temptation He (as in the past and is now and) will (always) provide the way out as well, so that you will be able to endure (without yielding and will overcome temptation with joy)."

Wow, I know that was a lot of fuel for you to filter into your fuel injectors but simply stated: If God brings you to it, Trust Him to bring you through it! He has pre-paved and made the way for you and me. What am I saying?

Some folks (spirits) are against your healing, your deliverance, your prosperity, your marriage, your beauty, your accomplishments, need I go on? They are ready to steal your joy, your hope and strength in Christ. Kill and bury your dreams and visions. So you have to stop living in the practical and live by the principles. Pray for discernment. Know what's of God and what's not; try the spirit by the spirit. Read the bible to study to show thyself approved unto God, a workman not ashamed of the Gospel but rightly dividing the word of truth 2 Tim 2:15; to know what's coming from the pulpit from the man or woman of God. Instead of spending half the day in astronomy or celestial study (pseudoscience) that leads you to dial Miss Psychic. Leave those Ouija boards and tarot cards alone and pull out your IPad to pull up your Daily Bread, for an inspiring TRUE word of God. Stop leaving your airways open and susceptible to robbery, abuts and destruction. Monitor your gateways. Turn on the praise station sometimes and leave it playing in your home when you are not there. Tune into a prayer conference line or good bible teaching and preaching TV program. The enemy is already programming those other channels. He or She or It is hosting those enticing (trick dawson) adds to those venues and free for all events to the lusts of the world, just to get you all caught up and set up to be victimized by something or someone. Don't let it happen.

D-Disarm

I love this instruction. You must take away the weapons of the enemy or his army (depending on the warfare). Sometimes it's a single attack and sometimes it's a battle. The definition of disarm means to Disable (put out of action) all his ammunition or devices. Make him helpless and surrender. Victory in the Spirit! Wow, am I the only one dancing right now? See you don't let the enemy think he has ammunition that is greater than yours. You have the full armor of God. Your armor is so powerful that when the enemy sees it, He already knows who your Chief in Commander is. The enemy already knows your Chief in Command has NEVER lost nor will lose a battle.

And although all we need to do is just, stand, we must know what tool to use in our armor belt. Like they say, you don't go to a shootout with a knife. Don't be so gullible and transparent to the enemy, when you actually should be transparent with God.

Reveal and acknowledge your weakness to God, the Father (he already knows) so you can be delivered, healed, restored and set free. Where you are weak, HE is strong!

What am I saying? Don't buy a Lucky 7, two dollar scratch off, when you know gambling is a weakness and it's a trigger to get you to spend all your money on the lotto, only to end up broke with bills to pay. Don't go to happy hour to meet colleagues when you are a recovering addict that's still struggling with the first step of admitting you have a problem. Don't hang out with the limelight single people at the singles club turning it up like you're single but opening yourself up to drama because you're actually married and should be on a date with your spouse or home with your spouse. We need to set up and install motion sensors called discernment and wisdom to recognize the signs of fox traps and kill tactics of the enemy intended to destroy your relationships, health and finances. The way a discerning mind demonstrates wisdom is it goes beyond the insight of what is seen and heard. God's word is 'spiritually' discerned. One example of this is right here in 1 Corinthians 2:14 "To the human mind without the Spirit, the things of God are foolishness. It's then the Holy Spirit that gives us spiritual discernment.

The bible also denotes in Proverbs 21:24 (NIV) that discernment has many collateral benefits. Let's examine the text. "My son, preserve sound judgment and discernment, do not let them out of your sight; they will be life for you, an ornament to grace your neck. Then you will go on your way in safety, and your foot will not stumble; when you lie down, you will not be afraid; when you lie down, your sleep will be sweet.

So don't be sucker punched and set up for the kill. Know where you are defeated. Suit up and expose the vices (spirits) and weaknesses (carnality). Call them out specifically by name. Ex. Drugs, greed, sex etc. in prayer.

Let me remind you about the Shepherd's protection for his sheep – Psalm 91 in the previous chapter, chapter 4. Security is of the one who Trusts in the Lord.

T-Transmit A Stronger Frequency.

Turn the enemy around. Confuse it (whatever your **IT** may be.) Redirect it, him or her from your territory! When you transmit something, it gives you the power to convey. It can be inherited or hereditary, but it's sent from one person to another with the cause or allowance to spread. A vivid illustration of this is in the book of Joshua 2:1-7; the story of Joshua and the Harlot Rahab.

We know the story well, but here is a snippet of transmission. There are two Israelite spies sent by Joshua to enter the city of Jericho to spy out the defenses of Jericho. The spies go to the house of Rahab, a prostitute. In lieu of her clemency and protection for her and her family's lives, she hides the spies from the king of Jericho and his messengers and lies to them, redirecting them from her territory telling the messengers, that the spies had already left. If you want to feel strong and protected you have to not only implement these instructions in your security system, but you have to be adamant about securing your territory. Here are the FREE tech support instructions after you install your A.D.T System:

You must speak to every one of your situations in life.

You have to get rid of some people, places and things.

You have to speak change (life) into your circumstances.

You have to praise your way through in faith to get your breakthrough.

You have to pray over your family, finances and your future.

You have to sow into your harvest with your time, talents and tithes.

You have to lay hands on yourself and plead the blood of Jesus and be healed by His stripes.

Do You Have an A.D.T system? Refer a friend. It has a Life time warranty and a lifetime guarantee and the system is FREE! No Fees, No contracts and includes the Free tech support instructions listed above!

Chapter 5: Scripture I Corinthians 15:58 (AMP)

[58] Therefore, my beloved brethren, be firm (steadfast), immovable, always abounding in the work of the Lord [always being superior, excelling, doing more than enough in the service of the Lord], knowing *and* being continually aware that your labor in the Lord is not futile [it is never wasted or to no purpose].

Chapter 5: R. A. W. for Christ's Kingdom.
Pardon Me, For Making Excuses

This scripture gives us specific detailed instructions of a R.A.W. worker for Christ.

By the end of this chapter you will clearly understand how to be R.A.W. for Christ's Kingdom, Amen!

R.A.W. (ready, able and willing). Your tenure in your walk with Christ and in Ministry should surely describe us to be the willing workers with R.A.W. ethics. We cannot be the living dead with a due expiration date. We must set our hearts not 'our minds' to have a PUSH and PULL lifestyle. Hear me, now! Minds can be manipulated, distracted & detoured, but the heart is what GOD sees. "I don't know about you, but what GOD sees is my primary concern. As I've said in the previous chapters, if God be for me, who can be against me!" REAL TALK… We've already acknowledged the signs of the times denote we are living in the last days. Nowadays, you rarely find relationships, businesses, or even memberships lasting 3yrs let alone 10, 20yrs… and if I can just strike a nerve… especially serving in the house of God for HIS kingdom. The excuses for not being RAW for Christ are endless. I've been in ministries where church folks leave because "The Pastor offended me, he could've said that to me personally," but all the Pastor did was preach a word that convicted you, so you leave the church.

OR, they didn't get to lead the song and drop out of the choir. OR, they weren't chosen to lead that ministry because they had a Degree so they sow discord and they begin church hopping. We Church folks are just such a fleshy mess. Oh but there is a GOD who sits high and looks low, A God of Love, forgiveness who is our present help in our Fleshy mess. We all need to Thank God and give Him some Glory.

I am so sure during any long tenure within a ministry there have been many unexpected, unpredictable, unexplained tasks and situations throughout the years.

However, just like the writer Paul, to be a willing workers you are persistent and don't allow anything to prevent oneself from being a RAW worker for Christ's kingdom for any longevity period of time in ministry.

This is how the subtitle, "Pardon Me for Making Excuses." of this chapter was derived: The Church of Corinth had many issues, and of course we can't relate here at your church, but they had a leader –Paul (Your Pastor) who taught them, guided them, encouraged them and set them straight when they wanted to go left instead of right.

Paul was the kind of disciple that would've been my BFF out of the whole crew of Apostles. Paul was Ride or Die! Down like 4 flat tires as a willing worker for Christ.

He was radical and high strung (full of energy) like me, before and after our conversions. Paul was persistent, fearless, and bold and had super human determination. He was strategic and intelligent. What he didn't know and what I didn't know was that GOD was going to turn our evil to good! He/I would be a Radical for Christ! Do we have any RADICALS for Christ reading this book? High five and a Shout out Hallelujah!

There is Good in Bad people, situations, and trials The mess you may be in right now, if you turn it over to the Master and toil that mustard seed of faith, Your Harvest of Victory, Healing, Finances, Deliverance, Breakthrough will manifest according to HIS riches and Glory! Come on Somebody… Believe it and Bless the Lord with me. Amen!

If Paul were here today, me and my BFF would be about that, "Just Do It" life. God said it; I believe it, just do it! Paul was R.A.W. with everyone throughout his journey. He just kept it 100 – always R.A.W. about his father's business. God used Paul in a supernatural way because Paul had the least experience with Christ, but did more with what he had.

Stop sizing and measuring yourself up with other folks. Don't stop planting your seeds for your vision, your business, your healing because someone else's crop is ripe for harvest and yours isn't YET!

We ALL have a season. Tend to your crop. Where your season may seem dormant now, it will manifest and become a ripe, overflowing harvest in your due Season. That's God's Promise! Pardon Me for making excuses…And because We don't stay on course with our vision. We don't ask God for clarity of our purpose. We don't Execute our talents or gifts, we abandon who we are. We stop planting, nourishing, and lose compassion for our harvest. We dry up and lose faith and ambition to press toward the mark of the high calling. We leave instead of cleave to ministry. We leave instead of cleave to the WORD of God, We leave the Church instead of cleave, thus limiting the legacy for ministry to prevail. The R.A.W. workers become extinct. We make excuses, like the old familiar ones below:

- We don't get up for church and if we have children we hinder them from stirring up there gifts/talents to be R.A.W. for Christ in Sunday School and Children's Church.

- We don't participate in ministry with our gifts/talents and therefore we are not being an inspiration to our children or our loved ones who come with us to service, to help them recognize and work their gifts in ministry. It all begins with US being living epistles read by men.

If you would, please allow me a Fox 5 Rick Camuto Business Moment:

The Dow Jones is losing again today with the R.A.W. Workers for the Kingdom of God. It has become the least favorable organization to get people to work steadfast and immovable. This Global KaTrillion Organization- The Kingdom of God- is the world's largest company. Owned by the Greatest and Richest Most Powerful entity in the nation known as Trinity Enterprise. The organization has the BEST benefits (a harvest plan) but the Employees (the laborers) are few. It's the only organization that gives promotions NOT demotions. It gives unlimited raises and bonuses (Favor and Grace) and has a humongous Employer match benefits program, the best of the nation (Blessings so abundant beyond what you could possibly think or imagine).

This organization never gives out pink slips, there's no racial discrimination, no nepotism, no layoffs, but this global organization just can't find anyone to work steadfast and immovable for Christ, the President of the Kingdom. The numerous Headquarters (Churches) are located all over the nation, and all of them are always hiring yet has the lowest employees of any organization. It is their policy, that No resume is ever refused! Everyone is guaranteed to get hired. But where are the R.A.W. Workers?

That's Business folks. I'm Rick Camuto, Fox 5 News… That's sad news, when On the other hand, our Blue Collar- White collar employees shine at work seldom making any excuses but only taking what's allowed (sick days, vacation days).

Whether our motive is for a promotion, a raise, or an employee of the month parking spot or even a plaque on the wall, we will attentively listen to the morning Pep Rally meetings, but fall asleep in service. We go to the company picnics, but miss the Church family picnic or any other fellowship event. We sign up for job trainings not even related to our job function but miss ministry rehearsals or empowerment workshops. We'll listen to boring hourly webinars but forget to call into Life Class. We'll even volunteer at the yearly company financial review but miss the church annual meeting. We can't even get folks to show up, let alone be on time, but we go above and beyond r the worldly job. We are so skillful at the art of making excuses, aren't we? Oh but let's get FREE today of Excuses. I was a PRO at Excuses… BEFORE I TRIED GOD A FEW TIMES and finally experienced the fullness of "Seek ye first the kingdom of God and all his righteous and everything will be added unto me!"   These were some of my excuses. See if any of these excuses sound familiar?

"It's the preacher's job." "It's not my gift." "I've already served, let someone else do it." "I'm too busy or too tired or too old or too young."

"I don't know if I'm ready yet?" "I don't have enough experience in that area." "This may require more than I'm able to provide." "They asking for volunteers on Saturday and I need to do me."

Hello somebody, if your job asked you to do something and you gave them an 'I'm not interested' excuse, I believe it would be called insubordination or just plain fired! I know I'm ringing somebody's doorbell, right now.

We pray daily and ask God to 'Use us or Have your way, Lord," but when he does call, we will make excuses, and start acting like Moses & Jeremiah. I'm going to use them as examples so I don't lose love with the Saints of God reading my book. These great men had more excuses than we could ever imagine, but for every excuse they had, God had a comeback: His Promise! "Excuses are tools of the incompetent, and those who specialize in them seldom go far." Ben Franklin wrote, "He that is good for making excuses is seldom good for anything else."

God gives us the gifts, the talents (we all know the parable of the talents), God fills us with the anointing, but we make up an excuse not to go R.A.W. for Christ and the Kingdom. We just find all sorts of excuses not to obey God's voice or be fishers of men.

Oh, hear me out Zion; God has little patience for the people's continual excuses and complaints, just as he did with Israel. Reread the track record of our forefathers. God has given us purpose and destiny. HE has given many examples of HIS perfection. God has moved in signs and wonders confirming HE is large and in charge. HE even sent HIS only begotten son to prove victory over death! We don't have to do anything in our own strength! Wow, Thank You Father.

Let's be Producers and Trust God to control every area of our lives. There are many unknowns to us, excuses shadowed in fear or just ignorance that we can be distracted by. Let's see.

Excuse #1- The Talent is too demanding. It requires too much thought and time.

Church announcement... We need a Leader/Director over a Ministry, not just a member of the ministry. We know we have the ability, but don't want the responsibility. Whatever the task God gives you, it's already a promotion that you are qualified for because of the talent you retain and He has already set up the provisions for you.

Jeremiah's calling was to be a Prophet, unlike his Father and Grandfather who were Priests. He too was a spokesperson for God, to declare God's Word to the people. He had a staff (priest) already in place to tend to the minor tasks. Jeremiah had to speak boldly and deliver messages to the present that had future ramifications. He had to expose the people's sins and call them back to their covenant responsibilities before God. Jeremiah's job as a prophet was unpredictable compared to a Priest because he never knew where God would send him or what he would say. The priests however were delegated by the written law. Priests ministered primarily to individuals with various needs. Prophets, on the other hand, addressed whole nations. Priests belonged to a special tribe and therefore had authority and respect, but a prophet could come from any tribe and had to prove his divine call. Priests were supported from the sacrifices and offerings of the people, but prophets had no guaranteed income.

People of God, God may assign you a demanding task, but his call keeps us going even when we don't want to go and are ready to quit. God is going to have HIS purpose fulfilled using us as vessels because he planned it that way, Jonah. We have the promise of God's purpose. He told Jeremiah in (Jer. 1:5).

"I chose you before I formed you in the womb; I set you apart before you were born'. (Repeat that verse again with me…

I mean Self Check here… This is a Paul moment for me! God Chose Me, & Set me apart! The Alpha & The Omega! Whew, Shut the front door! Anyone feeling a Praise in your spirit?

The phrases 'chose you' – 'formed you' – 'set you apart'- carries the recognition of the worth and purpose of him who is known. God knows you, chose you, and appointed you. Yes, Lawd I Thank You, Jesus!

You are known by name, hand-picked by God, and commissioned to serve. These acts give you and me a great sense of purpose. God's promise of his purpose within allows us to let go of our own plans and to receive HIS plan with NO fear.

Jesus didn't take authority over his future and he could've because HE is the Son of God. Therefore, we need to accept that our future is not our own. We are God's. He has a distinct plan and purpose for our lives. His plan is Dope! IJS. I read it again in Jeremiah 29:11. Then I did a self-check of the plans I have had for me. Sure enough, I choose burger king! It's better @ Lean not on your own understanding, but...

A second excuse: My talent is insufficient. I'm not good enough. I don't have a degree. I don't have any experience or knowledge in that area. That's not my expertise. Excuses, Excuses, Excuses! Moses & Jeremiah both felt like inadequate public speakers. Jeremiah told God (Jer. 1:6). "But I protested, 'Oh no, Lord, GOD! Look, I don't know how to speak since I am only a youth'" By the way, this excuse was shared by Moses (Ex. 4:10).

But Thanks Be to God, our Jehovah Jireh, who always provides a way to overcome weakness insufficiencies. When we are weak, HE is strong. When I was most aware of my own insufficiency is when I was most dependent on God being all sufficient. My own inabilities lead me to rely upon God. In my weakness, His strength is made perfect. Through my flaws His glory is manifested. Stop interviewing for God! He already made up his mind to hire you for the job when he chose your resume. Stop underestimating your talents ye of little faith. God always equips those he calls. He gives the instructions; we have his protection and the promise of God's provision. He did it for Jeremiah- (Jer. 1:9) and He will do it for you. He is the same GOD yesterday, today & tomorrow. When the LORD reached out His hand, touched his mouth, and told Jeremiah that he had filled his mouth with HIS words." The touch inspired and empowered Jeremiah. God has touched each and every one of US in some form or fashion. If we don't know, we need to ask HIM for a touch. Just a touch from you Lord, Ask Him what your gift, talent is or what purpose does he have for you to fulfill for the Kingdom. HE will show you!

It is not the most gifted and talented person that God uses, but it's the one touched by the hand of God. It's the most unlikely persons that God uses to shake the body of Christ, to shake a community and even shake a nation.

There is one thing I know for sure and that is NEVER underestimating the power of the touch; especially when God does the touching. How do I know? Because I'm a wretch saved by Grace. How do I know? Because the Bible tells me so... For all my "Show Me" folks reading this, let me share with you a few untouchables.

Noah was a drunk ~ Jacob was a liar ~ Joseph was abused ~ Moses stuttered ~ David was an adulterer and a murderer~ Elijah was suicidal~ Jonah ran from God~ need I go on?

Who can't GOD use? Which one are you? I had a combo, I'm just keeping it 100! Somebody tell somebody Pardon Me for Making Excuses.

I'm feeling another Paul Moment... The R.A.W. DEAL is... (Please, track with me), the People of GOD just don't believe what GOD has poured into them. We don't believe we can do all things through Christ, we don't believe, if God be for me, who can be against me. We don't believe bring the tithe/offering into the storehouse TRY ME and I will open up windows of heaven and pour out abundant blessings. We don't believe we can be a successful Entrepreneur, A Dr., Lawyer or Indian Chief. YET we go to Conferences, workshops, church Sunday after Sunday. We are happy and you know it for 1 hour in church and BOO, we get spooked by the trick of the enemy and back to not believing. We keep holding onto the past that creates fear and blockage for the future.

If we can't recognize the Christ within ourselves, no wonder we can't see it in others. We can't love one another and connect in the Spirit. Oh but if we walk in authority, we can see God's hand at work through us. That's a great place to Praise HIM. Let me suggest you reread chapter three about the DNA. We must recognize who & whose we are! We have the power and authority to put the enemy in his place. Jesus Christ gave ALL of US power and authority on that 3rd day. PRAISE GOD!

A common excuse: It's Not the Right Time. God says,' My time is not your time, nor my thoughts your thoughts.' The devil's busiest while is 'wait a while!'' Procrastination, the detour from your blessings.

Every time we set our minds to think not on these things… Every time we speak death instead of life from our mouths. Every time we don't receive the Word of God and hide it in our hearts, we stifle our blessings. That's why most of our blessings are delayed but not denied. Some have been held up a long, long time. Got cob webs and major dust on them but No expiration date. Whew, Thank You Father. Thank You God that your promise, Your WORD, is True and shall never return Void. That you have premeditated intentions to manifest in our lives, if we just be obedient, say Yes to become R.A.W. workers for the kingdom. Come on somebody, help me preach this morning!

Jeremiah whined, "I am only a youth" (Jer. 1:6). This verse denotes a young, unmarried man in his teens or early twenties. His response did not so much reveal his age but gave a deep sense of immaturity. So my spiritual instinct told me Jeremiah felt quite inferior, a bit inexperienced and very much intimidated by the size of the assignment God had summoned him to complete. I've been there and I am still challenged on some assignments and have that same feeling. Yet Zion, we must Be R.A.W.! It may be at any inopportune time that God calls us, but there will be foot prints in the sand. He will never send forth his servant alone. We have the promise of God's presence. Whom he predestined, them he also called, whom he calls, he justifies, whom he justifies, those also he glorified. He will never leave or forsake us. Just look for examples of the Lord's promise to be there. Expect HIS presence. Expect HIS promise to be fulfilled. Can anyone testify that 'HE's' an on time GOD?

Everything off the chain that God's voice has ever told me to do was a vital requirement or lifesaving experience. And every act of obedience giving HIM the glory HE Blessed me for it!

But, before I could experience God's presence, I had to go where God sent me, speak what God told me to say, and reject all fear. God does not give us a road map to follow, when he gives us an assignment. Nor does he leave us to our own resources. God walks with us through the entire ordeal, situation, project or task. We must be able to feel His presence which gives us the strength to stand in the face of every assault, just like Paul.

Better yet Jesus felt that same Presence. He and the Father were one. He could go on with the execution of an excruciating death because God walked with him. There is a great difference knowing when we are being sent, someone is going with us. Confidence, Support!

SO LETS GET RAW FOR CHRIST'S KINGDOM. NO MORE EXCUSES!

Hide (1 COR15:58) in your heart. Place it in your spiritual weapon's tool belt. In all our getting, let's get understanding! Be ye steadfast - Whatever may be the allusion, the sense is clear. Be firm, strong, and confident the strife, in the faith, in view of the truth that you will be raised up. Be not shaken or agitated with the temptations, and the cares of life. Be fixed in the faith, and let not the power of sin, or the arts of the enemy of the soul seduce you from the faith of the gospel.

(Hebrews 10:23) "Let us hold fast the confession of our hope without wavering, for He who promised is faithful.

Immovable –I thought that 'steadfast' and 'immovable' meant exactly the same thing, but there are key differences. Steadfast emphasizes the aspect of steadiness, while immovable emphasizes of faith in the gospel that will not be shaken even in the worst of circumstances. Paul was immovable. Always abounding in the work of the Lord - Always engaged in doing the will of God; in promoting his glory, and advancing his kingdom daily. The phrase means not only to be engaged in this, but to be engaged diligently, laboriously; excelling in this.

The "work of the Lord" here means that which the Lord requires; all the appropriate duties of Christians. Paul exhorts US to practice every Christian virtue, and to do all that we can do to further the gospel among people. We don't number or measure the work we do for God, we just abound in it always! (James 1:22) "But prove yourselves doers of the word, and not merely hearers who delude themselves. Knowing that your toil is not in vain in the Lord. You know it by the arguments which have been urged for the truth of the gospel; by your deep conviction that that gospel is true.

When we work for GOD, we are working for the best purpose we could ever find. It's a spiritual purpose, it's an eternal purpose, and it's a godly purpose. 2 Tim 1:12 reminds us.

"For this reason, I also suffer these things, but I am not ashamed; for I know whom I have believed and I am convinced that HE is able to guard what I have entrusted to HIM until that day."

Work for God will never be forgotten and the reward can never be equaled on earth. What is the reward? Eternal Life! The Kingdom needs SOLD OUT FOR CHRIST LABORERS... My heart is fixed, my mind's made up, no room, no vacancies, I'm all filled up His Spirit lives in me and that's the reason I'm souled out! Go Hard and Stay R.A.W. for Christ's Kingdom!

Chapter 6: Scripture- I Corinthians 3: 1-17 MSG

3 $^{1-4}$ But for right now friends, I'm completely frustrated by your unspiritual dealings with each other and with God. You're acting like infants in relation to Christ, capable of nothing much more than nursing at the breast. Well, then, I'll nurse you since you don't seem capable of anything more. As long as you grab for what makes you feel good or makes you look important, are you really much different than a babe at the breast, content only when everything's going your way? When one of you says, "I'm on Paul's side," and another says, "I'm for Apollos," aren't you being totally infantile?

$^{5-9}$ Who do you think Paul is, anyway? Or Apollos, for that matter? Servants, both of us—servants who waited on you as you gradually learned to entrust your lives to our mutual Master. We each carried out our servant assignment. I planted the seed, Apollos watered the plants, but *God* made you grow. It's not the one who plants or the one who waters who is at the center of this process but God, who makes things grow. Planting and watering are menial servant jobs at minimum wages. What makes them worth doing is the God we are serving. You happen to be God's field in which we are working.

$^{9-15}$ Or, to put it another way, you are God's house. Using the gift God gave me as a good architect, I designed blueprints; Apollos is putting up the walls. Let each carpenter who comes on the job take care to build on the foundation! Remember, there is only one foundation, the one already laid: Jesus Christ. Take particular care in picking out your building materials. Eventually there is going to be an inspection. If you use cheap or inferior materials, you'll be found out. The inspection will be thorough and rigorous. You won't get by with a thing. If your work passes inspection, fine; if it doesn't, your part of the building will be torn out and started over. But *you* won't be torn out; you'll survive— but just barely.

[16-17] You realize, don't you, that you are the temple of God, and God himself is present in you? No one will get by with vandalizing God's temple, you can be sure of that. God's temple is sacred—and you, remember, *are* the temple.

Chapter 6: Are You B.U.I.L.T. For This?

Are you B.U.I.L.T. for this was downloaded through me while I was studying to speak for the theme, "Building the House Together like Back in the Day." This instantly gave me a throwback of my childhood rearing. I share with you throughout this book a lot of my testimonies and experiences. I believe this helps build a relationship with you and me; and you, me and God. My back in the day picture became vivid: A native Trinidadian; skinny minnie, caramel coated little girl with two pigtails and colorful barrettes in my hair, adopted to live in USA. From third world country villages to Spring Garden Street Projects in Philadelphia, PA.

Whether village or projects, there was a sense of peace and living at leisure in the neighborhood community. You recall, I shared that, we didn't lock our doors at night, we could actually leave them open all hours of the night. The residents in the projects were descendants from the founding generations that were raised there since the projects were established. So the neighborhood was the watch; the village that raised the child. Yes, in the projects everyone knew what each child's name was and who were their parents and 95% the family's grandparent's names. They knew who moved in and who moved out. Oh, and when it was time for church, Lawd have mercy on my soul. Everybody and I mean everybody, unless sick or shut in went to church and was always there on time. You would serve wherever there was a need, and no one was exempt. Children were taught to serve at walking/talking age. So when it was time for revivals, regardless if it was your church or not (as they were all related one way or another), you attended to serve and support the neighborhood community churches. It was true; when you heard the older, seasoned saints talk about churchin from sun up to sun down. We stayed in the house of the Lawd and we all were with one accord.

What I remember most was if there was an ought between brothers or sisters, those church folk knew about it and the elders, especially the church mothers, would get it straight. You didn't have to worry about it leaving outside those four walls of the church.

The next thing you knew, the church mother or deacon, depending on who had the ought, male or female, was bringing both parties together for the talk. You knew then if you had any other scheduled plans they were definitely cancelled, because this was a sermon lesson learned workshop combined. The last reconciling resort was the Pastor. If it went to the Pastor, it definitely best not leak out to the other community legacy churches about the issues going on inside the individual legacy church. The elders didn't tolerate church gossip. No one was going to say that the Cushites church was not a church of order or Christ's agape love. This non-tolerated action would cause the other church folks in the community not to come to the events of your church, out of embarrassment and the lacking of agape love. Yep, if you couldn't settle things within your house (church family) and it got out to the community, that was not a good thing and it definitely didn't sit well with the Leaders and the Pastors.

This was the laid basic church and community foundation back in the day. The Ole School Saints setting the Ole School ways of character, integrity and respect. Each carrying its own equivalent weight and were all mandatory. So as I reflect on today, I ask myself 'Where did those same rooted principles from back in the day go? The same principles established from the same basic biblical foundation, Jesus Christ. We read daily about the church growth and see the buildings going up but the Christians, the actual church of bible believers are decreasing in power. How could this be when we have the advanced access of God's word via social media, TV programs, and church buildings on every corner? Conferences every week going on throughout the nation, strong leadership teaching/training and umpteen translations of the bible? So why are we not all more mature in the Christian walk, in our faith as a church family?

Instead of building our church family, we, the church, are scattering and dividing. Vastly losing ourselves and our members of the body of Christ to the world. We, us, the Church actually have the most obstacles in the Christian community. Why is that? I am so glad you asked. The answer is simple, we don't reinforce our foundations. We don't accept diversity in ministry and we won't unify in purpose. We have no humility in spirit and we are definitely not acting like we're mature in the knowledge of God.

Therefore, our structure is not built on the solid rock, Jesus Christ! Another throwback… You remember the ole church sang this hymn…

My hope is built on nothing less
Than Jesus' blood and righteousness;
I dare not trust the sweetest frame,
But wholly lean on Jesus' name.

On Christ, the solid Rock, I stand;
All other ground is sinking sand, All other ground is sinking sand.

Yes, even the hymns had stamina and virtue. There's a saying that we say, 'been there done that with t-shirts to prove it.' Well just in case you all don't see it in the spiritual, you definitely can see it in the natural; that is we have the same cultural and congregational issues that went on in Corinth, only difference is ours are escalated because of the era we live in, yet we are acting no different. Yep, go ahead and agree. It's the truth and you might have witnessed something just recently at your own church. Father, help us today!

Yes, I know as human beings we have dysfunctions and disagreements within our family. I can admit, because I am a 'special' child of God at Mt. Sinai, my own church. However, we cannot allow personal prejudices or sectarianism (narrow-mindedness) or denomination clicks within the church because both are carnal and lead us into spiritual infidelity. If we are in the state of spiritual infidelity, we become no earthly good, because we abandon the love of God and our relationship with Him. Good Lord, we can't be the 21st Century Corinthians!

How does the world keep progressing, while the church is digressing? Would it be because we are so busy acting like earthly folks (unsaved), that we forget we were ever spiritual (saved)? Then we encounter the **'GRESSION'** Spirit… **REGRESSION** (Put that old man back on.) One foot in and one foot out; doing people, places and things. One foot in **DEPRESSION** (sitting on the famous woe is me bench) yet filled with anger, bitterness and guilt. I just need a Praise break right here. Oh, but Thank You Father God, that your love for us is unconditional! How you look beyond our faults and see our needs.

How you forgive us and not forget us, that you gave us your son, Jesus Christ, so we can get back on the mission of **SUBMISSION** to your will for our lives and the plans that you have for each of us! I truly hope someone reading felt that in their ShaNaNa and gave God some Glory!

So then ask yourself, '**Are You B.U.I.L.T for This?** Well, let's do a building inspection. I am going to use my biblical imagination and examine with you the letter of Paul to the Corinthians finding the violations that causes division within Church. We will then cross examine the 21st Century Corinthians church in order to reinforce our structure. Like all engineers and building contractors we must have a strong foundation. (I Corinthians 3:1-4) Paul (your Pastor) is the spiritual Father for the Church of Corinth (your church). He's raising the King's Kids with the Word of God (life classes, sun worship, bible studies, and leadership meetings) but at this point is a bit ticked off, because he can't speak and communicate to them at their level of maturity due to their immature childlike actions. My biblical imaginative eyes see Paul shouting (All caps in his letter) "Hello Corinth! Just in case you have forgotten as it appears by your unscrupulous behavior, all of you make up the local church and are a church family. We have discussed this many times, so get yourselves together.

How can you sit in service, take three pages of notes from the sermon and before you get out the door, sow discord? How can you come up for prayer and go sit back down in the pew, with the same desire to sin? Why are you still coming to the ministry meetings and the church meetings with the same hater aide for your leader and/or the members in your ministry?

All this time (months/years) you've been a church family member here in Corinth and I've been preaching to you and teaching on spiritual principles from the word of God. I've read and reviewed with you all the bible stories and given you the biblical doctrines, yet you are acting like you don't have a foundation in Christ. You have gone from All Star mature Christians (feeding on the word and allowing the Holy Spirit to direct your paths) to wholly (entirely/fully) immature carnal Christians. Talk to me, Zion.

We as believers must manage conflicts inside the church with the ole school spiritual principles; not stir up controversy and misbehavior. Let's be real right now. It is not the walls of the church building, or the doors to the building nor is it the parking lot we pull up into to get inside the church building, but it is us, the church. We are the folks talking, acting and covered in carnality. We offend the non-believer as well as the believers. Do you not recall, that the carnal nature is 'us' BEFORE we met Christ. (Reread Romans 7:14) Do you not have in the notes you wrote reminding us that we must choose to walk according to the spirit, not the flesh? (Reread Roman 8:1) Did you not buy the CD from the message, Carnal Chaos-Romans 8:7-8; when I said to all of you, "The carnal mind is enmity (hostility, hatred) against God?" For it is not subject to the law of God, not indeed can be. So those who are in the flesh cannot please God! Listen to me Corinth, I repeat! We fight spiritual battles with spiritual weapons, not carnal ones. Paul didn't call you Babes in Christ as a compliment; he was referring to your state of immaturity. Put the bottle down and reach back for your cup! Don't stop growing in grace. Put on the mind of Christ and live by the spirit of God. Stop being governed by mere natural instincts; lean not on your own understanding.

I am here to tell you something about the bottle, it's capped off! There is nothing coming out of the nipple anymore. We can't let the word of God and the works of God sit inside of you dormant or dead. Wake Up. Rise Up and reach for your cup. Let your cup run over with the abundance of God. Keep pouring into your cup. I asked God, "What's up with this cup?" The Holy Spirit responded," **The container adds value to the contents."** I recall telling you I was Special (personality) in my own church, so I answered back in an acute tone of voice in my living room, walking around my stone living room table," Wait, Holy Spirit. I am missing something. Show me more about the container adding value to the contents, please. Well, there was silence just like a phone gone dead. I kept repeating, the container adds value to the contents over and over. It wasn't long before I received an illumination. The cup in the bible signifies **Spiritual Truth.** The truth of faith, which is from the good of charity.

I researched a few scriptures in the bible commentary with the word cup in it that also pertained to the biblical significance and jotted them down with more explanation to help deliver the revelation of God's word.

Jehovah, thou wilt set in order a table before me in the presence of mine enemies; thou wilt make fat my head with oil; my cup will run over (psalm 23:5)

In this text, to set in order a table and anoint the head with oil denotes being gifted with the good of charity and love; my cup will run over denotes that the natural is thence filled with the spiritual truth and good.

What shall I render unto Jehovah? I will take the cup of salvation, and call upon the name of Jehovah (psalm 116: 12-13)

In this text, to take the cup of salvation denotes the appropriation of the goods of faith.

Lastly from the gospel of Mark- *Whosoever shall give you drink in a cup of water in My name, because ye are Christ's, verily I say unto you, he shall not lose his reward (Mark 9:41)*

In this text, to give drink in a cup of water in my name denotes instructing in the truths of faith from a little charity.

Wow! That's deep. I kept reading the text and the biblical meaning. I kept repeating 'the container adds value to the contents and I heard the Holy Spirit whisper. He said If God can get the outside to radiate the faith on the inside, and then no sinful nature or any devil in hell can cause oneself to become a double minded man, let alone a worldly carnal Christian.

The more we drink from the cup (truths of faith) filling ourselves with the word of God on the inside, it will seep through our pores and God can use you and me to attract another soul to be saved by grace. How's that? I asked, trying to keep a dialogue with the HS. But instead of a conversation, I instantly got the vision. The more you drink from the cup that contains the truths of faith with the word of God we become full and content (peace).

Your contentment on the inside will glow on the outside. You will feel in your hands, feel it in your feet, and feel Him all over and in you. The aura, your looks, your walk, your talk, smile and bubbling joy will compel the lost. And then when we all assemble together, it will set the atmosphere for His presence.

Daily, we must let the spiritual truth of faith fill us with more of You Lord, on the inside. As you look in the mirror, fill your cup with, "I can do all things through Christ that strengthens me. Recognize that you are fearfully and wonderfully made in his likeness and image. There's a song I love written by Sounds of Blackness and the lyrics say...

"I got a message from above, you ain't no thug, you're Royalty!

Brother you're a King, Sister You're a Queen, we're children of the tree,

If you've never been told, time for You to know... You're Royalty! Marvelous, Powerful.

We can't stop growing. It's faith that builds a strong foundation to build the kingdom which only comes with the knowledge of God. Now that we have the foundation solidified, we can begin building the structure. (Diversity in ministry) Paul goes on in verses 5-8 and points out the importance for diversity in ministry. We really need to accept diversity in ministry. We all individually make up the field (church) and according to our labor will reap the harvest. Kingdom people need to be cultivating the soil, sowing seed, watering the plants so they bear good fruit. All of us should be Street Generals out Soul Winning!

My Pawpaw and Nana had farms and were also farm laborers for large fruit and vegetable industries. I would watch as Pawpaw cultivated the ground before he planted the seeds. Then he would fertilize the soil with manure, then water. In reading the verses, the word cultivating came to the forefront of my mind, so I went to Google and found this Mantis Farming website and read this explanation:

"Nature takes a toll on the soil as the elements actively dry it into a crust. Cultivating breaks up the crusty soil surface allowing for a much easier penetration of air, nutrients and water deep into the soil where plant roots can gain access to them.

While almost everyone knows the importance of water to a garden, it is vital that air is able to penetrate the soil surface in order to benefit the micro-organisms in the soil that perform the various important tasks of improving the soil and creating nutrients for plants. Cultivating the soil also makes it easier for newly germinated seeds to sprout through the surface of the soil."

IMMEDIATELY, the NATAPH downloaded. Read the paragraph again. This time as the revelation, reading with the parenthetical words.

"Nature (WORLD) takes a toll on the soil (SOUL) as the elements (SALVATION) actively dry it into a crust (FLESH). Cultivating(MINISTRIES) breaks up the crusty soil (CARNAL SOUL) surface allowing for a much easier penetration of air (PRAISE/WORSHIP), nutrients (TESTIMONIES) and water (WORD OF GOD) deep into the soil (SOUL) where plant roots (FAITH) can gain access to them. While almost everyone knows the importance of water (WORD OF GOD) to a garden (BODY OF CHRIST), it is vital that air (HOLY SPIRIT) is able to penetrate the soil (SOUL) also makes it easier for newly germinated seeds (CONVERTS) to sprout through the surface of the soil (SOUL).

My God, My God! God is Awesome! God created us all different, with exceptional talents (gifts) to fulfill his purpose in the kingdom. The bible clearly speaks of diversity in 1 Corinthians 12: 4-11 (NKJV)

[4] There are diversities of gifts, but the same Spirit. [5] There are differences of ministries, but the same Lord. [6] And there are diversities of activities, but it is the same God who works all in all. [7] But the manifestation of the Spirit is given to each one for the profit of all: [8] for to one is given the word of wisdom through the Spirit, to another the word of knowledge through the same Spirit, [9] to another faith by the same Spirit, to another gifts of healings by the same[b] Spirit, [10] to another the working of miracles, to another prophecy, to another discerning of spirits, to another different kinds of tongues, to another

the interpretation of tongues. [11] But one and the same Spirit works all these things, distributing to each one individually as He wills.

I know I can't sing, but I like to sing because I am a Praiser. To me, I sound real good, until I'm so into me thinking I am Jekalyn Carr. Our worship leader and my sister Elder Prophetess Etoyi will give me that; 'Please sing SoLo look! SoLo that no one can hear you. She will never hand me the mic because she knows my praise is not always in key with the musicians. I try to sneak a moment by picking up the mic as if it is an accident, while the worship is high in the atmosphere, and get caught every time, with another "You better not" look. I get it and receive the correction in love, so I laugh and continue to praise and worship the Lord. Now I would do very well in the choir with my fellow brothers and sisters as we unify (operative word) in melody but I am not a lead singer. What am I saying? Study, get training and perfect your gift. Here is the diversity in ministry: **It's ALL about JESUS!** Each ministry has a part to do in the field (church) in order to produce fruit for the harvest to see manifest in the kingdom of God. God so heartily agrees. Read verses 12-14, where the word makes it plain about the Body of Christ and the members.

Diversity can cause division, when there are few violations in the inspection of the structure. You will find the same members in the ministry always laboring (don't grow weary-Isaiah). This violation occurs when there is an overflow of Pew Planters in the Church that want to stay on the bottle and not reach for their cup and work their gift. Therefore; they are not contributing to the work in the kingdom and fulfilling their God given purpose. These pew planters have taken the spiritual gift assessment test at least six times and still not in a ministry. So now they're stagnate in the state of lack (finances, opportunities) because they do not trust the promises of God and how the gift will make room for them before great men.

Or you may have the Dip Laborers that joined a ministry just to say they belong to a ministry, yet dip out before rehearsal if they ever make the rehearsal at all. They dip from the schedule of duty (make excuses every time to serve) but always complaining or criticizing. The most common diversity violation that causes division is not having unity in purpose among the laborers and the leaders.

The common factor here is no matter what the work is or who has to do the work, it's all for the Glory of God.

There should be no big I or little U. If we can just stop spending so much time trying to outdo our brother or sister and unify in the spirit as (1) Body, we would be so anointed and powerful. We all have a vital function in God's plan. One will plant, one will water but each will receive his own reward according to his own labor. Honestly, neither of the individual efforts amount to an Emmy or Oscar winning effort. But as my mentor says, "It works so much better, when we do it together!"

Lastly, this violation needs to cease quickly; no humility in Spirit. God has ordained all of us to be ministers of the Gospel on earth (cultivators) but he gives the increase. It is not by works, so no man can boast (Ephesians 2:9). If God's not getting the glory, there should be no boasting of the story. So, Sir/Madam please check your motives. Glorifying anything beyond God is a carnal deed. If God's blessings are not a part of any outside effort, then its failure. So check yourself before you wreck yourself. Look for the 'Well done, not I got it done.' The Church is the construction site. The congregation (each believer) is the builder. The bible is the blueprint and the Holy Spirit (dwells within) is the onsite architect, who guides us as to when, where and how to build. We build into the church what we build into our own lives (the quality of materials). The more we tear down our lives we fail to build values into the church that will last, like back in the day. We may look successful on the outside, but once again dying of spiritual infidelity on the inside. Please protect your gateways. We fight to maintain our salvation every day from the enemy and his tactics. This is all the more reason to build on your foundation with strong quality materials (Prayer, Fasting, and Power of the Spirit)

Now I ask you, 'Are You B.U.I.L.T. for this? The answer is Yes, I am all because of Jesus. He…

B- Bought With A Price. I Peter 1:5 (KJV)

"Who are kept by the power of God through faith unto salvation ready to be revealed in the last time."

70

U-Upholds Us. Psalm 145: 14 (KJV)

"The LORD upholdeth all that fall, and raiseth up all those that be bowed down."

I –Intercessor. Hebrews 7:25 (KJV)

[25] Wherefore he is able also to save them to the uttermost that comes unto God by him, seeing he ever liveth to make intercession for them.

L- Loves Unconditionally. Romans 8:37-39(KJV)

[37] Nay, in all these things we are more than conquerors through him that loved us.[38] For I am persuaded, that neither death, nor life, nor angels, nor principalities, nor powers, nor things present, nor things to come,[39] Nor height, nor depth, nor any other creature, shall be able to separate us from the love of God, which is in Christ Jesus our Lord.

T-Trust Him. Psalm 37:3(NKJV)

[3] Trust in the LORD, and do good; so shalt thou dwell in the land, and verily thou shalt be fed.

Chapter 7- Scripture   Ephesians 4: 1-5 (AMP)

4 So I, the prisoner for the Lord, appeal to you to live a life worthy of the calling to which you have been called [that is, to live a life that exhibits godly character, moral courage, personal integrity, and mature behavior—a life that expresses gratitude to God for your salvation], [2] with all humility [forsaking self-righteousness], and gentleness [maintaining self-control], with patience, bearing with one another [a]in [unselfish] love. [3] Make every effort to keep the oneness of the Spirit in the bond of peace [each individual working together to make the whole successful]. [4] *There is* one body [of believers] and one Spirit—just as you were called to one hope when called [to salvation]. [5] one Lord, one faith, one baptism,

Footnotes:

1. Ephesians 4:2 The key to understanding this and other statements about love is to know that this love (the Greek word *agape*) is not so much a matter of emotion as it is of doing things for the benefit of another person, that is, having an unselfish concern for another and a willingness to seek the best for another.

Chapter 7. R.I.S.E. U.P. ZION!

Paul is whom I consider a ride or die Apostle that deals with doctrine of the Church as the Body of Christ in the first three prior chapters in Ephesus. Paul was intentional about explaining the importance of unity and he knew the revelation of the Church as the Body of Christ was crucial to understanding God's marvelous plan of working in and through His people to accomplish His worldwide eternal purpose. So Paul sets the momentum and the tone for the church of Ephesus.

Paul tells us about spiritual possession in chapters 1 (1:1-14). He then goes to tell us about spiritual position in chapters (2 and 3). So here we are in Chapter four, where Paul is elaborating on "Unity and connecting".   Unity being an actual duty and responsibility of the church because of the blessings we enjoy in the prior chapters: spiritual possessions and spiritual positions. We have this unity/connection in Christ by virtue because of His work on the cross at Calvary. Jesus reconciled both the Jew and the Gentiles to God! So that is why today, I want to say to the people of God…" R.I.S.E U.P. Zion" Rise Up!

We have all heard this slogan advertised by the astounding actor Samuel Jackson. This phrase causes momentum of the Atlanta fans and the Atlanta Falcons, to be with one accord, to connect and unify. The driven force to be with one accord and unify escalates the brotherhood and sisterhood in the stadium, home, bar, restaurant, tavern or where ever you may be watching the game. It unifies and directs the synergy to fulfill one purpose- VICTORY. Rise up echoing in the stadium increases the adrenaline of the Atlanta Falcons and ignites sparks of energy to win the game. It creates unity and one common goal or purpose in each player's ability syndicated to rise up and win! The rise up activates all the falcon fans to have the same mindset, heart and passion to support the team and believe they can win. The Falcons work together as a TEAM, in spite of their positions on the field, size, height, race, color, creed or religion.

Each player uses their own skill (calling) on the football field under the play given by the coach that's lead by the quarter back to execute. Regardless of what else is going on in their personal lives, what may be happening in the crowd, or even with the opposition of the other team, when it's time to R.I.S.E. U.P., they are all unified to do one thing and that's their best to win.

We the church need to R.I.S.E U.P. and celebrate the unity of being one body in Christ to be victorious in the spirit! It's our time to reap and redeem everything that God has already promised. Paul is in prison, but he gets the word from his friend Epaphras (lovely) who helped him establish the Colossian church when problems were going on within the Colossae Church.

Just a FYI, don't ever think for one moment that folks don't hear about the mess going on in the four walls of (your) church. How can I say that? Because we, the church create mess, bring mess, spread mess and then leave a mess. Then we wonder why folks don't want to come to our church to visit, let alone join. We have to R.I.S.E U.P. Zion. There are many types of Christians, but being a discord disciple is not an acceptable option.

So Paul writes this letter to Ephesus (preventive maintenance of the Colossae mess spreading) as it was the 2nd largest city in the Roman Empire as well as a hub for other regional churches. He sends this letter by way of Tychicus, who was a faithful minister/servant during Paul's 1st Roman imprisonment to deliver. Paul's impassioned prayer about the church that was written in chapter two is now taken to a deeper level and challenge of what we, the church is called to do and that is to live a worthy Christian life. It is not enough that it is God's intent for us, the church to one body in Christ, but it is up to us; you and me; Us as in We to unify and connect with each other and be people in unity of the Holy Spirit through the bond of peace day by day.

Queen Latifah said it best; UNITY, it's a Unity! Somebody shout, "it's time to RISE UP!" So how do we R.I.S.E. U.P.? I am so glad you asked.

R- Respect Your Leadership.

Paul describes this in the book of Ephesians that gifted leaders are given to keep the church on target (v7-10). The Greek word 'Dogmata' is used here rather than the word 'Charismata' to describe sign and service gifts granted to individuals. I referenced this in Romans 12:1 and I Corinthians 12. Let me say this again respectfully but with a strong tone. Your Bishop, Pastor or Apostle is a gift given to your church. The Holy Spirit knows and follows orders given by God. **KNOW YOUR LEADER!** We are all leaders in the kingdom of God and need to act as such. It is written whom God predestined, He called, He justified and He glorified. You must be teachable so you can be the BEST you can be in your spiritual position/calling. We are most effective to the body of Christ, when we are in the right place. Understand your assignment for the Kingdom of God. Know your purpose. There is a time and a season and everyone has one. Atlanta Falcons are a prime example. It took them 25 years and the remnant is redeemed to make it to the Super bowl. Don't go ahead of your season. God will strategically plant people in your life to help you on your journey. Whatever you do, please don't be a discord disciple in your church. If you can't take instructions from your leader, then try a church up the street around the corner up the block, where you can be the boss of the hot sauce before you sow discord and cause division and separation, which is against the duty and responsibility of the church. Instead, look in the mirror and see what the real issue may be. Then have a little talk with Jesus who is always on standby to listen.

I- Inspire One Another

When we each understand that we ALL are King's Kids, going back to Ephesians chapters one and two, we are affirmed to all be heirs of greatness and royal inheritance from the seed of Abraham. (Deuteronomy 28: 1-6). We all have been blessed with a measure of grace, gifts and talents. So what are you doing with yours? Don't hate on your brother or sister's glory, you don't know their story.

If you have not discovered your gift or have a vision with revelation blueprinted by the Holy Spirit, then support- sow (there goes that word again) into your brother or sister who does have a vision. Start with your Pastor! Support the vision and mission of your church. This is the best investment on earth, because you will ALWAYS get the BEST return. There is never a bad Dow Jones day.

Real Talk... We sow into people's visions every day that we don't know, that don't labor among us without strife or hesitation. People who don't personally pray for you, care for you or know you, they are just doing Customer Service because you are growing their vision. Who and where you ask? Nail shop, Starbucks, shopping mall, to name a few. Yet, when we look at the other end of the spectrum, it's a big issue to support or sow into your brother or sister (their business or side hobby hustle) that you labor among and break bread with in the body of Christ. Sometimes we won't even speak to each other, just walk right by, rolling our eyeballs and thinking thoughts that would burn hell wide open. Oh, help us Lord! Teach us to Love one another like you love.

S-Sow

We don't get anything if we give nothing. The foundation comes before the walls. The gospel writer John reminds us, God gave his only begotten son for our salvation. We can't top that, and God doesn't ask for human or animal sacrifices anymore. He wants your stewardship. Hold, handle and hand over God's goods as He sees fit. The harvest doesn't become plentiful until you plant something. We all know the scripture in Malachi 3:10: Bring the tithes, talents and time to the storehouse, so there will be meat in your house.

Stop picking out your neighbor's garden. You must plant seed for your own garden- your own vision, your own healing, your ministry and your legacy. If there is no demand for the supply, then create it. Stop generalizing and go specific. If you are a sower, trust God! If I could tell all of my testimonies of giving and how God blessed the seed, it would be a very long sequel of novels. God said," Try me and see if He will not pour you out a harvest so abundant, you will not have room enough to receive." That heavenly bank account NEVER runs out of Blessings, Grace and Favor. Wait I say on the Lord! So put the treasure on the same righteous podium with a sacred motive.

I want you to plant this deep in your spirit and that is 'we all have a season of harvest.' So tend to your crop. If your crop seems dormant now, it will manifest and be a ripe overflowing harvest in your due season. That's God's promise! Stay committed to God's ministry. Work your measure! Increase your talent. Bring your gift up to excellent standards (I Cor 10:31)

Turn up your **S.W.A.G. (Service- Worship-Accountability-Giving)** and watch your harvest overflow.

E- Examine Your Heart

Why are you attached to certain folks? What's your motive? What's the connection or is there actually any? What are your motives to receive your blessings? Do you have a Gehazi Spirit?

What did you just say, Dr. Bailey? Well, so glad you asked. When you connect with people with a heart for God, we do it in love. We do it out of concern and passion for a Soul's salvation as Christ. We seek ye first the kingdom of God and all his righteousness according to his riches and glory (Matthew 6:33) my favorite scripture. We don't use our name and influence to get ahead and especially not behind your brother or sister's back. We don't use the ministry for material things and handouts for our own personal gain. In other words, we don't 'Pimp the Church.' Stop roleplaying a position that's not yours (operating in the wrong calling) because you want recognition or don't know what your calling is to get the proper training. Don't use authority that you don't have, taking liberties out of order and causing confusion. Paul reminds us in verses 14-16 of Ephesians, that we don't compromise our values. We connect with people in the kingdom and represent Christ when we put off the old self and put on the new self. Let flesh and stuff not prevail over God's will and way.

U-Unify

It is very clear in verse 4 to not be selfish. The society we live in is a very self-oriented society. The big question we ask when we have a decision to make, whether to do something or not is, "What's in it for me?" or "How will I benefit from this?"

However, Christ's Church is not selfish. As a Christian, the question should be, "How can this benefit the Kingdom of God?"

President JFK once said, 'Ask not what your country can do for you, but what you can do for your country." And if that is true of something like an earthly political establishment, how much more true should it be of Christians and the kingdom of God? We need to spend less time thinking of what God and what the Church can offer us and spend more time asking God what can we do for Him and His Church. Here are few helpful hints: Spend more time in prayer interceding. Stop sitting on your anointing in the pews and put it into action in the ministry. Sacrifice some of your Saturday time and be a street general in the Evangelism and Outreach ministry. Be on time for meetings, classes and rehearsals. Stop complaining about things, suggestions, processes etc. Become a part of the solution and not the problem especially if you are in leadership.

Self is all about the individual, but the kingdom is about the body of Christ. God's intended church isn't made up of a lot of disconnected people, yours and mine maybe, but it shouldn't be. The church is not you over there doing your thing and me over here doing my thing. Just imagine your body parts deciding not to work together. I believe we all want to fulfill God's purpose in this life. But if we allow ourselves to become selfish, then we end up doing our own thing. It's not that we don't want to do God's work, but we just don't want to do it with brother so and so or sister so and so. Well get over it. Put your differences to rest or bury them. This is not accomplishing anything for the kingdom, this is separating the kingdom. Iron sharpens iron. We, the church must work together. When we diminish the importance of unity in the body of Christ, we risk being invaded by the enemy.

The disciples had to go forth and spread the gospel to the entire world. We are the NOW generation of disciples to fulfill the Great Commission.

P-Prepare

Prepare to praise God. Prepare to worship. Prepare to know God! Prepare to be about your Father's business. Prepare for elevation in HIM. Prepare for revelations to be revealed to you.

Nourish the power of the Holy Spirit in your life, because it is our source to restore inability. Get intimate with the Holy Spirit and you will discover the fullness of God. Prepare for an overflow harvest. Prepare for the Prophetic to manifest in your life. Prepare to provoke God to Bless you. Blessings are of God they come with a process and a price to pay. Just because they may be delayed, doesn't mean they are denied. Prepare to remain stirred for the Kingdom of God via daily devotion, daily journals and speaking in tongues daily in prayer. Prepare to be sold out for Christ! Walk in the spirit and you will not fulfill the lusts of the flesh. Relax in His presence. Trust in His timing. Rely on His promise. Wait for His answer. Rejoice in His boldness! **R.I.S.E. U.P. Zion!**

Chapter 8: Scripture 1 PETER 2:4-10 (NKJV)

[4] Coming to Him *as to* a living stone, rejected indeed by men, but chosen by God *and* precious, [5] you also, as living stones, are being built up a spiritual house, a holy priesthood, to offer up spiritual sacrifices acceptable to God through Jesus Christ. [6] Therefore it is also contained in the Scripture, "Behold, I lay in Zion, A chief cornerstone, elect, precious, And he who believes on Him will by no means be put to shame."[7] Therefore, to you who believe, *He is* precious; but to those who are disobedient, "The stone which the builders rejected, has become the chief cornerstone," [8] and "A stone of stumbling, and a rock of offense." They stumble, being disobedient to the word, to which they also were appointed. [9] But you *are* a chosen generation, a royal priesthood, a holy nation, His own special people, that you may proclaim the praises of Him who called you out of darkness into His marvelous light; [10] who once *were* not a people but *are* now the people of God, who had not obtained mercy but now have obtained mercy.

Chapter 8: G.E.M.S.T.O.N.E: What type are YOU?

I love this epistle by Simon Peter. Being an APD –Apostolic Petrine Disciple, I find that I have more in common with Peter than Paul. For instance: Peter was a committed disciple first of all. Him Andrew left everything they had without a second thought to follow Jesus! (Luke 5:9-1). Peter's favorite weapon of choice was the knife (a sword back then) as is mine (any kind of blade) upgraded to the 2 edged sword; the Word of God. Peter was teachable, had faith and He believed in his Master Teacher: Matthew16:15-16; He said to them, "But who do you say that I am?"[16] Simon Peter answered and said, "You are the Christ, the Son of the living God."

Peter was true to his calling; So much he was ordained by God to be the Rock to build the Church! "[17] Jesus answered and said to him, "Blessed are you, Simon Bar-Jonah, for flesh and blood has not revealed *this* to you, but My Father who is in heaven. [18] And I also say to you that you are Peter, and on this rock I will build my church, and the gates of Hades shall not prevail against it. Peter was consistent… when he was scared, he was scared. He stuck to his story… denied Christ (3) times, Peter wasn't going to be crucified. He was true to the game not the players.

Lastly, after his last instructions, Apostle Peter was a bold witness for the faith. He knew his identity in Christ. He knew what his purpose was for the kingdom. How many of you are RIDE or DIE to the calling on your life? Can God trust you to be all you can be with the Gifts you have to build the Church? Wow, that was so good and I haven't even introduced this chapter. So the title of this chapter is G.E.M.S.T.O.N.E: What type are YOU?

If I were to ask you, what is your gemstone, would you be able to tell me without hesitation? What if I asked you, what is your birthstone? You would probably be more familiar with that word and answer expediently, yet the birthstone is of less value than the gemstone because of its association?

Gem stones are made with minerals VS Birthstones are a type of the twelve gemstones traditionally associated with the month of one's birth. Any of a similar list of less costly substitutes. We church folks must be very careful of our association. Be in the world not of the world. Don't let your good be spoken for evil. Hang with the eagles & leave those pigeons alone. We are not Nevertheless; but above and not beneath. The head and not the tail. Know who you are & whose you are?

A gemstone (also called a gem, fine gem, jewel, precious stone or semi-precious stone) is a piece of mineral crystal which, in cut and polished form, is used to make jewelry or other adornments. However, certain rocks (such as lapis lazuli) or organic materials that are not minerals (such as amber, jet, and pearl) are also used for jewelry and are therefore often considered to be gemstones (birthstone) as well. Most gemstones are hard, but some soft minerals are used in jewelry because of their luster or other physical properties that have aesthetic value. Rarity is another characteristic that lends value to a gemstone. Apart from jewelry, from earliest antiquity engraved gems and hardstone carvings, such as cups, were major luxury art forms.

Don't be a vessel with value and only serve with a limited purpose. We are Christ's G.E.M.S.T.O.N.E: (God's Embellished Masterpieces Sanctified Treasures Optimizing Nobel Ecclesia) (a precious or semiprecious stone, especially one cut, polished by Jesus the lapidary, used to build the Church! We must know our True Identity in Christ. What type of gemstone are you?

In this letter, Peter is speaking to a bunch of struggling Christians going through trials and being pressed against the wall of exterior circumstances, and have lost their identity. A group, whose message rings out best to me from Grandmaster Flash & the Furious Five: *Don't push me cause I'm close to the edge, I'm trying not to lose my head, it's like a jungle sometimes, it makes me wonder how I keep from going under!*

Come on somebody, have you not been at this place… short on cash, don't have no stash, & your car empty with gas. Cant' get ahead for the setback situations. Can't get a dollar from the person that owes you $10.

Can't get a decent conversation because everybody is stressed and burdens are eating at their wits end just like you, or at least they are perpetrating to be so you don't ask them for nothing. This breaks, that aches and Oh for Goodness Sakes... You just forget who 'You' really are and Whose you really are! You forget this too shall pass. You forget I can do all things. You forget HE is my rock & my fortress. You forget I'm a King's kid and my Daddy owns it all, and all I have to do is TRY HIM and SEE if he won't open the windows of heaven and pour me out a Blessing! Glory to God!

So Peter is in Woodruff Park speaking to the people who are considered nobodies or homeless. Some have lost their jobs, some their homes. Others thrown out of their families. Some controlled by drugs, alcohol & prostitution. Although though they know Jehovah, they feel like a worthless nobody as if the events in their life were/ are totally beyond their control. BUT how many of you know...BELIEVE... that NOTHING's too hard for GOD! Hallelujah! I don't care where you are, HE will meet you! I don't care how bad it looks, HE is Able to do exceedingly & abundantly above all you can possibly imagine or ask. Hallelujah... Praise the ALMighty God you serve right at this very moment! Peter had to let them know they were G.E.M.S.T.O.N.E.S. referred here as Living Stones that were a part of the Great cornerstone. He explains two basic things in this passage to help us discover our true identity.

The first, We must be enveloped in Christ's identity: When we read the text in verses 4-8, It is obvious we need to back off long enough from our woe is me daily existence to realize that we're not just a replica or substitute gem. But we are rare, precious stones. God is at work building a beautiful tabernacle and house and temple in us and through us.

Look at how Peter uses the illustration of Christ as the Stone. When I asked my husband about using stones in construction, he said that stones can be used to brace, fit, support or stand for something that is stable and gives foundation. Peter's illustration in verses (4-8) calls Christ, the Living Stone. Now, we all know that stones don't have life, but Peter is using the Irony to paint a picture.

Check out the irony in the OT (Exodus 17 and Numbers 20), where twice we find Israel in the wilderness experience being without water. Both times Moses took a rod & struck the rock and water came out. God provided living water for his people then, and Christ is the living Rock that was smitten, crucified and provided life for us in the NT. Yes, Jesus Christ is our living stone (rock in OT) in the midst of hardship and stress. Coming to Christ we receive life and sustenance! The True blessing is it's not a one-time visit, but a perpetual process of continual coming to HIM. We can confess our sins and repent and Jesus, who sits at the right hand of the Father, intercedes for US. Grace and Mercy is shed in remission of our sin. Trial or not, we must continue to build the Christ within us. We must continue to rely on our foundation (cornerstone) of our lives. We must continue to inherit the minerals, rocklike stability of love, hope, forgiveness, peace, joy, faith that makes us HIS G.E.M.S.T.O.N.E.S. (living stones) to build the kingdom of God. We must continue to make Christ the center of our life. We do not want to be a certain rock with organic materials that are not minerals dba a birthstone. A stone stumbling and rejected because of disbelief and not embracing Christ in your life. God is our refuge, our redeemer, where we dwell in the secret place and under the shadow of the Most High. God always provides himself as sanctuary for those who put their trust in HIM. We gemstones (living stones) with our rocklike DNA used to build up God's spiritual house. There's a place for you and me in the body of Christ. There's a purpose for you and me to fulfill. We are G.E.M.S.T.O.N.E.S.! Don't let your gemstone fall out the crown!

So how do we develop G.E.M.S.T.O.N.E. **(God's Embellished Masterpieces Sanctified Treasures Optimizing Nobel Ecclesia)** Identity? Let's go back to Peter's epistle and hear what he describes our gemstone identity to be. In verse nine there is a plethora of noble characteristics of being a King's Kid. Peter begins saying you are the acceptable "chosen race".

"You are the ones chosen by God . . . from nothing to something, from rejected to accepted" (1 Peter 2:9-10, The Message). Most of us spend our entire life trying to earn acceptance. It begins with our parents, and then we seek it from our peers and later from our partners.

We will even go so far as to seek acceptance from the people we envy and of course the people we respect. The desire to be accepted is so relevant; the influence is reflected in the kind of clothes we wear, the kind of car we drive, the kind of house we buy, and even the career we choose. So here's a question: Why are we so driven by acceptance? This is easy, because human beings love the feeling of acceptance. We love to know that someone has chosen and accepted us. He goes on to say you are valuable because you are "God's people for His possession".

Let's keep it real. When you are chosen, accepted, it does something for your self-esteem. It actually raises your self-esteem. Sometimes we even get the helium head, rooster chest and a peacock stroll. I'm Just Sayin. But seriously, how much do you think you are worth? Although Accounting is my profession, I am not talking about net worth surprisingly, but I am talking about self-worth. Hear me clearly, there is something we should NEVER do and that is to confuse valuables with value as a person. That's not acceptable.

Before getting to the question, how much do you think you are worth? Let me ask you what determines value? So now, I am going to implement the financial side of me to give you a clear detailed answer. There are two things that determine value in life: Value depends on what someone is willing to pay for something. Things like a house and a car; they are only worth whatever someone is willing to pay for them. And material value depends on who has owned the item in the past. Based on these two criteria, now I ask you the question again, what's your value? How much are you worth? The Scripture says, "You have been bought and paid for by Christ, so you belong to him" (1 Cor. 7:23 NIV). Who owns you? What was paid for you? Jesus Christ owns you and paid for you with his life. Hallelujah! Our Father exchanged his only begotten Son for you and me. The cross at Calvary proves your value. God the Father says "I love you this much". An unconditional Love! Agape Love! Jesus Christ gave his life for you and me. And Jesus didn't die for junk. Let that resonate in your ShaNaNa for a minute. I don't think we ever really truly contemplate the Love God has for each of us even at our lowest, dirtiest, ugliest, darkest, sinful state. Even in all of that, one cannot begin to comprehend the incredible worth we are to Jesus.

If we were to go to a Gemologist and get appraised using society's value system, we may seem like nothing more than amber, in comparison to a diamond. But to Jesus, we are the most valuable rare and extremely precious treasure in the entire world.

This is what opened my eyes. You are capable "a royal priesthood". Peter referred to us as a priest. What he was saying here is that the two benefits that priests have are now available to everybody who is a believer in Jesus Christ. You have direct access to God. We can go directly to God for ourselves. We don't have to pray through anyone else. We don't have to confess our sins to anyone else. We don't have to experience God through anyone else. We can go directly to God for ourselves. Ministering to the needs of other people is our responsibility. Every Christian is a minister. We are not pastors, but ministers. God's word says that you and I have been gifted for ministry to serve other people. "God's instruments to do his work and speak out for him, to tell others of the night-and-day difference he made for us" (1 Peter 2:9, The Message).

'Sacerdos' is the Latin word for priest, which means bridge. The priest is a bridge builder between God and man. I've heard old preachers say it this way, "We are saved to serve." If we are not serving what in the world were we saved for? Are you a bit more excited about your purpose in the Kingdom now? Are you truly feeling the esteem because GOD has entrusted his work to you and me? Finally, where would we be without this mineral? You are forgivable. You and I are forgiven. There are no three words that communicate self-worth better than: You are forgiven. I am so glad Our Father is not like our Brother or Sister. I mean, God doesn't rub your sins in, he rubs them out. God will not rehearse your sin, like we do, HE releases it. The ABC of Salvation: Admit you are a sinner. Believe in Jesus. Confess that Jesus is your Lord. He wipes away our sins; they are forgotten; gone; erased; cast in the sea of forgiveness as though they never existed. God's unconditional love for us puts HIM in the business of forgiving sin. He takes all our sins and wipes our slate clean. Creates in us a clean heart. Immediately, our past is purged. This is God's mercy and grace. When we confess and repent of our sin, Christ forgives us immediately and without charge.

So there you have it. G.E.M.S.T.O.N.E. - **(God's Embellished Masterpieces Sanctified Treasures Optimizing Nobel Ecclesia)** what type are you?

I am acceptable. I am valuable. I am capable. I am forgivable. God has done all this for us, "so that you may proclaim the praises of the One who called you out of darkness into His marvelous light" (1 Peter 2:9). Know Who & Whose You Are! We are God's handiwork, his masterpiece and his creation. Let's give God a Shabach of Praise! Hallelujah! Thank You Jesus. The scripture says, "Once you were not a people, but now you are God's people; you had not received mercy, but now you have received mercy" (1 Peter 2:10). We are King's Kids - we are chosen, we have worth, we are found capable, we are forgiven. Now that we have and believe that, it doesn't matter what the world's judging system says. God didn't make NO JUNK. God too reminds us in various books of the bible that we are his children, if we trust and believe in Him. We may rebel and abuse our rights and privileges, but God still tells us that we are His. Thank You, Lord God!

There is NOBODY LIKE YOU!

Chapter 9: Scripture – Psalm 104:4

O LORD my God, You are very great:
You are clothed with honor and majesty,
[2] Who cover *Yourself* with light as *with* a garment,
Who stretch out the heavens like a curtain.

[3] He lays the beams of His upper chambers in the waters,
Who makes the clouds His chariot,
Who walks on the wings of the wind,
[4] Who makes His angels spirits,
His ministers a flame of fire.

Chapter 9: Women on F. I. R. E.!
Watch My Smoke While I Burn

I wanted to dedicate this chapter to my Positive Life Chapel International family in Ghana, Accra. The Women on Fire Conference 2017 was explosive with the power of the Holy Spirit and the presence of GOD!

We all need to keep our F.I.R.E. burning for Jesus. There is something about the fire shut up in your bones that never needs to cease burning. Why your flames need to keep burning! Why your fire should never flicker and go out. What your fire does for you in your life. In psalm 104:4, the angels are the spiritual ministers to God and we are the earthly ministers to God. We wait for and listen to his orders then we execute them because of the burning love we have for God, for Christ and the Kingdom, not to mention the flaming zeal for God's cause and interest.

So go with me on this imagery journey to turn up the heat of this F.I.R.E. Each letter in the word 'FIRE' is representing a flame that will turn up the degree of the fire. In the USA, the degrees determine the severity of a fire. For example, Women on F.I.R.E. will be a four alarm fire. This means this blaze is more difficult to handle than a two or three alarm fire. You with me so far? The higher the degree, the higher your flames, the more firefighters (angels) are dispatched to battle the blaze. I feel a praise about to burst out in these flames. The first flame.

F- Fulfill Your Purpose!

God created each and every one of you with a purpose. He designed you to carry. We carry and bring life into the world. Birth your vision. Be true to your calling. Walk in your destiny and accomplish your goals. What is the passion that burns inside of you, that you are called to do for the kingdom of God and prosper as your soul prospers?

Some may not know your purpose, and that's okay too because all you have to do is go before God and ask, "Lord, show me my purpose?" 'What is my gift that will bring me before great men?' Please, make sure you are ready to receive and embrace what He reveals to you. Don't keep looking at your current situation and stay there. Don't be your own stumbling block. In you is beauty. Each and every woman reading this is fearfully and wonderfully made. Grab a hold of God's unchanging hand. There is power in the touch, especially when God does the touching. I can't reiterate these examples in the bible enough, but it's real. Just know that our ancestors really and truly have 'been there, done that and left us the t-shirts to prove it'. Lol.

~ Naomi was a widow~ Job went bankrupt ~ John the Baptist ate bugs ~ Peter denied Christ ~ Martha worried about everything ~ The Samaritan woman was divorced *(more than once)* ~ Zacchaeus was too small ~ Timothy had an ulcer ~ Lazarus was dead!

So who can't God use? Those that are dabbling in witchcraft stop it or you are going to burn in your own flames. I don't know who that's going to help, but believe the word of God.

Birth your Vision and follow your dreams. You can be that doctor, famous musician, author, wealthy business entrepreneur. Whatever you set your heart and mind to be, you can do all things… The second flame.

I – Intercede For Spiritual Blessings

It is better to give than to receive, especially when it comes to giving of yourself in prayer. We are truly blessed to be chosen to be the only creatures to have an open communication with God the Father, through his son Jesus Christ with our own intercessor the Holy Spirit. What a mighty sovereign God we serve. God is so awesome to care for us and love us like He does. He makes sure we are always protected and he is always available. When you give of yourself in prayer for others' deliverance, healing, restoration, it brings you closer to our Father. Most importantly, we will know His voice. We know who we are to Him and Who He is in us.

You will be blessed with an increase of power and anointing as you open your mouth to pray or lay hands to heal. Even before Jesus was crucified to fulfill his purpose and die for our sins, he went to Gethsemane (Matthew 26: 36-46) to pray and intercede for us. He even took three of the disciples with him to teach them to watch and pray, so they too would be blessed (rewarded openly for what they do secretly) Although the disciples grew weary and fell asleep more than once, Jesus still prayed and covered them also.

Go into your secret place and hide in His tabernacle. Whenever your enemy pursues you, God will keep you safe from harm. Wherever your war room is or whenever it's your time to be a watchman on the wall, don't get weary in well doing like the disciples. We know that the spirit is willing but the flesh is weak, that's why it's so vital to keep your zeal for God. It's so good to know that there were a few women on fire in the bible, who blazed the trail before you and me. We can always refer back to the bible and study these women to sharpen our prayer life and our faith, besides God is the same God yesterday, today and tomorrow, whom answered these women's prayers and will answer ours.

- **Anna** used her strength in prayer and fasting- Luke 2:37

- **Hannah** prayed fervently- 1 Samuel 1:10

- **Junia** was a missionary- Romans16:7

- **The woman at the well** helped win her city to Christ- John 4:39

- **Rahab** the harlot gathered her family to safety- Joshua 6:23-25

- **Philip's daughters** preached the gospel- Acts 21:8-9

- **Tabitha** was a disciple (student) and had a ministry of helps making coats for widows- Acts 9:36-39

- **Phoebe** was a helper in the Lord- Romans- 16:1-2

- **Women** ministered unto Christ of their substance- Luke 8:3

- **Mary** anointed Jesus with ointment very precious- John 12:3

- **The widow** gave of her want- Luke 21:2

- **Another Mary** gave support for the man of God for the Lord- Romans 16:6

- **Mary the anointer** sat at the feet of Jesus and heard His word- Luke 10:39

- **Priscilla** ministered for the Lord with her husband Aquila- Romans 16:3-4

- **Tryphena and Tryphosa** laboured for the Lord- Romans 16:12

Wow, many prayer warriors! Greater is he that is in you, than he that is in the world. The third flame…

R – Rejoice and Give Thanks

There is power in your praise. David said, "Let everything that have breath, praise ye the Lord" (psalm 150:6). Praise will get you to the throne of grace. A grace that abounds more than sin. A grace that is sufficient. His power is made perfect in weakness. It gets even greater because where there is grace (praise), there is mercy (worship)! Oh how great is God's favor and God's presence; Oh, Hallelujah to the King of Kings. We all know and often say, "Favor ain't fair" but it sure feels good. Well when the enemy comes in like a flood, the spirit of God will raise a standard against Him. (Isaiah 59:19). God will call his army to stop the enemy. Oh is anybody praising God right now to scatter and flee their enemies? Open up your mouth and Shabach the Lord for me. Thank Ya. When you open your mouth or wave your hands or do a dance or sing a song of praise, the victory in the spirit prevails. The trumpet of Zion is sounded. The walls will fall and breakthrough will rush in. The enemy knows this sound, therefore the weapons that formed, will not prosper against you! When praises go up, the blessings come down. If God be for you who can be against you? Get your praise on! The fourth flame…

E- Expect Great Things From Your Fire!

The flames are high and burning real hot now! It's an out of control four alarm fire! You are walking in your purpose. You are praying for others and have an intimate closer relationship with God. You are rejoicing and praising in faith, power and authority. You can be sure that your flames are going to burn down everything that is not of God in your life! Sickness in your body, depression, lack of finances, havoc in your home, promotion on your job, a healthier marriage. Everything the enemy set out to destroy you will burn and become smoke. The smoke goes up in the clouds; those are your issues ascending up into the heavens, because the timber is built on Jesus Christ. The same Christ who has descended into hell, defeated Satan, freed the captives and then rose like smoke and ascended and sits by the right hand of God the Father. His smoke paid it all for You and Me! Stay on F.I.R.E and watch your smoke while you burn!

Chapter 10: Scripture   Romans 13:1-7 (NKJV)

13 Let every soul be subject to the governing authorities. For there is no authority except from God, and the authorities that exist are appointed by God. [2] Therefore whoever resists the authority resists the ordinance of God and those who resist will bring judgment on themselves. [3] For rulers are not a terror to good works, but to evil. Do you want to be unafraid of the authority? Do what is good, and you will have praise from the same. [4] For he is God's minister to you for good. But if you do evil, be afraid; for he does not bear the sword in vain; for he is God's minister, an avenger to *execute* wrath on him who practices evil. [5] Therefore *you* must be subject, not only because of wrath but also for conscience' sake. [6] For because of this you also pay taxes, for they are God's ministers attending continually to this very thing.

[7] Render therefore to all their due: taxes to whom taxes *are due,* customs to whom customs, fear to whom fear, honor to whom honor.

Chapter 10: WHOSE H.O.U.S.E. IS THIS?

I don't know about you but I have thousands of journals. I never go anywhere without something to write on besides a store receipt or the back of a flyer etc. So this day as I was preparing to study and prepare a word for the theme, 'Take Care of God's Shepherds', the voice of God was long winded and very precise when he said to me, "Don't worry about my shepherds, as they are protected in the shadows of the most high. Tell my people to take care of me." So, I said, "Excuse me God, I don't mean to question or be out of order, but you are GOD. You are the great I AM, so sir you don't need any help. If anything, you need your people to stay out of your way of trying to help you." He said, "My people do not reverence me as God. They do not even reverence my house, therefore how will they reverence my shepherds?

What is going on in the natural is an indicator of the spiritual malfunction. Teach and speak to my people about spiritual authority."

God is no joke. After I read Romans 13: 1-7, I had an immediate flash back in the natural of my NanaMa-Ruth, whom Yall call Big Mama. My Big Mama, Ruth was a hefty solid black foot – Seminole Indian, African American that absolutely took no stuff. She would look at you and stare with that eye which meant, try me if you want to. She would back slap you quicker than the wind could blow if you smart mouthed her. She had the mindset: Do what I say; I brought your mama here, so I will take you out. She also had a heart bigger than the Atlantic. No one was ever hungry because she cooked huge restaurant pots for the community. No one was without a roof over their heads because she owned 21 properties throughout Philadelphia and a huge home in Atlantic City, NJ, so she had a room for anybody. No one was without a means to provide because she would always put you to work doing something and would pay you. Everyone in the community near and far, knew and loved Mrs. Ruth.

At Big Mama's house, there were rules and it didn't matter if you were 2, 12, 22 or 62, everyone respected her authority. She reigned with a rod of respect and integrity. At Big Mama's house you knew: to wipe your feet outside, pull your shoes off at the edge of the door.

No smoking in her house. If you sleep in or on it, you make it up. If you eat off it, you clean it up. If you wear it, hang it up. If you open it, then close it. What you did at your house, your auntie's house, you did not do at Big Mama's house. The most powerful sign of authority is reflected because she didn't' have to be home in the house and everyone still abided by the rules and whomever she left to watch over her house, you still respected that person as authority in her place. You could still feel her presence, see her face and hear her voice in your mind.

God is saying the same to us today. Paul teaches in this same lesson. Let's just flow here a minute. Authority is real. We are subject to various types of authority daily. You have Expert authority, like being a professor (authority on a subject) or a Gymnast, (authority in a chosen field.) You have Tyrant/Dictator authority which is acquired through coercion, abuse or manipulation. You also have Delegated authority. Pastors delegate to leaders and members, your boss may delegate to you or if you are in a management position, you delegate to your staff. Last but not least you have entrusted authority. This is our police or elected officials that are entrusted by society to protect or enforce laws and seek the best interest of the people. Above all of these types of authorities, there is the #1 authority and that is GOD. God's authority is First! The fact remains, that it is the church that God chooses to manifest his authority, better known as Spiritual Authority. The bible says, "All authority in heaven and earth has been given to me." (Matthew 28:18) And just because our Father is so gracious to give us freedom of choice, meaning a permissive will or a perfect will, let's not get it twisted, there is no other authority that has any latitude over God. God is the ULTIMATE authority. God also chooses his authority to be seen in his Shepherds (Pastors) as well as in the body of Christ (church). So if we examine the text, would you agree with me that, our God is a God of order and not the author of confusion?

God's extreme case of **'OCD'** (Order-Clarity- Divinity) caused the importance of his authority to establish order here on the earth, and ordained entirely by God Himself. God establishes the (3) Spheres or institutions of authority on earth by means of the home and family first. This consists of the husband, wife and children.

(Read Gen 2:18-25). Then the government, that being national leaders, local officials and citizens (Read Gen 9: 1-7). Finally, the best was saved for last, the Church. This includes all of our church leaders and the fivefold ministry (Read Acts 2). When the Bible speaks about spiritual authority, it's actually connecting, relating or referring to God establishing offices or positions of authority within the church, the body of Christ illuminated by the five fold. Christians relate best to the office of Pastor/Teacher. Do you know why this is recognized as one office? Simply because a Pastor should also be able to teach, but every teacher is not able to Pastor. Whew, I know I am talking right in this sentence. When we celebrate Shepherds as Pastor/Teachers, we see the disciples Peter and Timothy also referred to them as Elder's and Overseers (I Peter 5:1-4 and I Timothy 3: 1-7). The Pastor's ordinance of express purpose is to prepare God's people for kingdom service and help them mature in the faith. As servants, we should all want to be found faithful when Christ returns. Pastors are chosen for the calling, divinely equipped and given the responsibility to teach and preach, care for and lead the sheep delegated by Christ himself.

Nugget Drops: * When God chooses us for His calling, we must obey and follow; No Exceptions! God will bring about what he purposes, ask Jonah*

*God chooses Pastors, they didn't choose God (John 15:16). Unlike being called and not chosen. (Matthew 22:14). Let me show you the difference. Being chosen for the calling means, you accepted the invitation to be a Pastor and comply with the conditions as a lifestyle (Grace of Faith, Holiness and Love) verses accepting a position or office of Pastor to only participate in the kingdom of God with limited convenience and standards. If you have a problem with your Pastor, You have a problem with God!

Whose H.O.U.S.E. Is This? This is God's House! Each one of us represents God. He dwells within. We should be able to recognize our own kinsmen. We assemble together Wednesdays, Sundays and whatever other days of the week, and we become the body of Christ (name of your church or ministry) representing God and being led by God's (your) wonderful Pastor.

This is how we tie the spiritual authority in reverence to God. These are "Big Daddy's" housekeeping rules for your house:

H- Have Respect for Your House

A house divided against itself will not stand. (Matthew 12:25) Yes we will have disagreements, what family doesn't, but let's not disgrace your ministry (family name). A family that's in constant squabble disintegrates. You are either with God or against God. You are either going to follow the Godly principles set by God; instructed and executed by the chosen instructor (Pastor) or sabotage yourself to Satan's set up for destruction. You are either going to support the vision and build up the mission for the specific house of God or be banished from the blessings that God has for this house.

O-Offer to Help

Our only motive as Christians should be the love of Christ in our hearts. Love supersedes, conquers and covers all. (Philippians 2:1-4) Showing love for others, will eliminate sin against our brother or sister. There's a difference between unity and uniformity. True spiritual unity comes from within, because it is a matter of the heart. Uniformity on the other hand, is the result of pressure from without, disagreements. If there are a lot of disagreements in a ministry, then this strongly denotes that there are spiritual problems in your fellowship and the only solution is to get your hearts right with Christ and then with each other.

Father God, I bind the spirit of selfishness and pride, right now in the mighty name of Jesus. Christians need to really understand the meaning of 'humility' in the bible. I read this quote from Andrew Murray and I found it to be deep and it checked me.

"A Humble person is not one who thinks meanly of himself; he simple doesn't think of himself at all."

If you are truly humble, you know and accept yourself. Romans 12:3 paraphrased. In other words, you yield yourself to Christ to be a servant to use. You use what you are and what you have for the Glory of God and for the good of others. The operative word is 'others'. So let me clarify my statement. This doesn't mean you are at the beck and call of everybody to become a religious doormat for all to step on and wipe their feet upon and be used all the time. This is not what I mean at all. Nor am I saying that you are to buy friendship or positions in church or become the Preacher's pet. Just giving in and saying 'Yes' to everybody's whim. No Sir, No Ma'am! You are however; a servant for Jesus sake, Amen!

U-Understand Those Who Labor Over You In Your House.

When your Pastor is in the will of God, teaching you the true sound doctrine from the bible, a REMA word of God for your life that dwells in your ShaNaNa; fasts and prays and ministers to you with or without appointments; cares for you and your family members (known and unknown); cares about your well-being; preaches and teaches not just to run a program; he or she is not a hireling just for the paycheck and benefits; defends their sheep when outside attacks the fold, It's without a shadow of a doubt that you should obey, cover in prayer and support your spiritual leader(s). We're not in church but that's a good place to give God praise!

And the real '411' '911'- God's word says," The results of a disobedient Christian are unprofitable: (useless, serving no purpose, mis-improving talents and bringing no glory to God) not for the Pastor, but for yourself. The Pastors, they serve out of the loyalty to the relationship with God and the sheep not from the expectation for the reward. The relationship with Christ has royal values and inherited relationship based on the grace of the master not the servant's worth.

S- SET EXAMPLE IN YOUR HOUSE.

We don't worship people or give them glory, but let's give honor where honor is due as it pertains to their faithful work as paraphrased in Hebrews 13:7. We are so blessed to be able to read books, listen to CD's or watch videos of our current and past great leaders for a refueling of the word of God. As a believer, I listen to, or purchase products from and even sit under my leader and Bishop to see the evidence of their fruits and imitate their faith.

99

What's working for my Bishop Dr. David E Jackson, Apostle Dr. Gloria Holden, Apostle France Collins, Joel Olsteen, and Bishop TD Jakes in the faith is what I want to happen in my life.

Their lives are pointed to Christ and Christ is the center of their Faith. So don't hate on a Pastor's glory or anyone else's, you don't know their story. We are to build our faith on nothing less but Jesus Christ. HE never changes. Jesus Christ the same, yesterday, today and tomorrow.

E- ENJOY YOUR FAMILY

Family begins with your own home (church). You would be a very ineffectual church in the community, when there is disarray under your own roof. As a total stranger, if I can't feel and discern true love and the presence of God in your house (church), then you more than likely would be talkin, but ain't sayin nothing to me, as the late James Brown would put it. I would just be courteous acting like I'm listening with tunnel ear, going in one and out the other.

Make preparation to meet a need! A family works together to make sure all needs are met. Everything we need is in the body of Christ. Support and sow into one another! This builds your house. Learn each other's character, skills, talents and gifts. If we are not caring for or providing for your house, your family, then someone has denied the faith. Faith is the outer expression of the Love of God in us. He commands us to show love to the world, so how can we show love to the world if we don't learn to first demonstrate love to all those at home in our house?

Whose H.O.U.S.E. Is This?

Chapter 11: The Chosen R.E.M.N.A.N.T….

FAVOR IS FAIR!

Hello there! In order for you to vividly flow with me to understand this chapter, and receive the impartation that's definitely going to bless you…You must have a spirit of expectation. You must be totally transparent with yourself and open to the Holy Spirit as you read on. On the real skinny, God already knows, so one might as well be TRUE to SELF & TRUE to GOD.

My prayer for you as you read," The Chosen Remnant… Favor is Fair." is that you develop a genuine spirit of "Use Me Lord!" Become eagerly on fire; mind, body & soul with infinite energy to be about Our Father's business as declared in the GREAT COMMISSION! Matthew 28:16

It is truly amazing how the old cliché, "saving the best for last" is a powerful and effective saying which still holds true and has relevant meaning today. I'm speaking specifically about the word Remnant in the title which will be spelled out in acronym, later on in the passage. We all know the meaning of the word chosen, but just for clarity, I've gone to Merriam (Webster dictionary that is) for the definition.

Chosen: An elect person or one who is the object of choice or divine favor.

So, if I'm chosen, I have favor. Wow, that puts a notch on my belt and inspires me to turn up my SWAG (Service. Worship. Accountability. Giving,) that's a whole other message. But the key word in the title is the word *'remnant'.* I am a testimony of being a Chosen Remnant! Just like the people of Jerusalem in Zechariah the seventh (7th) chapter, I was totally disobedient & rebellious. I put the C in carnal minded and it separated me from God.

[11] "But they refused to heed, shrugged their shoulders, and stopped their ears so that they could not hear. [12] Yes, they made their hearts like flint, refusing to hear the law and the words which the LORD of hosts

had sent by His Spirit through the former prophets. Thus great wrath came from the LORD of hosts. [13] Therefore it happened, that just as He proclaimed and they would not hear, so they called out and I would not listen," says the LORD of hosts. Zechariah 7: 11-13.

SIN was IN! The world and all the hell it brought was exciting to me, so I foolishly thought. I am still digging deep, filtering and scanning my life, of the self-destruction memory videos. The only difference now is, I'm using my VIP (**Victory In Prayer**) preventive maintenance system that I totally disregarded then, because I was disobedient & rebellious. I was just adamant about doing me and my thing in the world. The thoughts and feelings that once contaminated my heart, mind & soul, now has an internal alert called, discernment through the Holy Spirit. Back in the day, the enemy was So Pleased with how I destroyed my life. I Mocked God, messed up my credit worthiness and my reputation and distorted my character. I became a dreg and menace to society, mistaking all my good for bad and then a permanent resident of LoDaBar. My family abandoned me and I deserted them. I was disconnected from the source of life which is GOD the Father!

Here me when I say, "It's by God's grace & mercy that I am alive!" HE will indeed fulfill HIS purpose through You and get the Glory; regardless of how disobedient, defiant, rebellious, reluctant, trifling or succumbed in the world of sin you may be! Whatever the state, God can and will use You!

Okay, let me share my testimony with you.

I am adopted and was brought to the states (Philadelphia), by my birth mother's best friend who became my mother, the only mother I knew. At 54, I still don't know my biological parents. I was told my mother was from Trinidad (Port of Spain), my dad, Cuban, was military and I was a mistake. I was raised in Catholic school but went to church with my Baptist grandmothers all my life. I lived in the projects of Philadelphia, but my adopted parents worked hard.

We moved to Lawnside, NJ when I was 10. My Mother was part of a strong religious, intelligent, loving yet dysfunctional voodoo working family (NanaMa (grandma) Ruth) & my father was a hardworking alcoholic agnostic, because his father (Rev. Harvey) was a hypocritical preacher. He would constantly tell me, under the influence, "I would be nothing when I grew up." I later found out I was adopted at 15 and there began my spiral of disobedience, rebellion & living hell.

I ran away at 15 & was arrested (turned myself in because my NanaMa Ruth said I should). The courts opened Pandora's Box. The pain and anger was so intense, that I openly told the judge, "I didn't want to go back to what was home, because these were not my parents." My adopted mother cried! I had hurt her in spite of all she did for me. I didn't care now. It was revenge & rebellion. I chose to live with NanaMa Ruth in Philadelphia. At 16, I graduated from high school class valedictorian then became pregnant at 16 ½ after the prom. This is another place of healing in my life. Yes, I was seduced by my mother's step brother, my NanaMa's God son, who was trusted to Chaperone me to the prom. What they didn't know behind the scenes was that he preyed and watched me grow up with the intent of taking my virginity. A baby having a baby, I had no value of being a mother and my mindset was that I didn't really have one.

I felt my adopted mother had lied to me all those years. It began make sense, my adopted father kept sabotaging my mind and saying that I would be nothing, because I wasn't his real daughter. My NanaMa Ruth became my world and just like the bible story of Ruth & Naomi, I would never leave her. She finished raising me into a woman and began raising my son, her great grandson. A year later, while at Thomas Jefferson University, studying to be a medical laboratory technologist, I was introduced to marijuana by my son's father (Orthodox Muslim & a biker). Now I'm a dealer of mary jane and pills while hanging out at biker's clubs. I dropped out of Thomas Jefferson University, now practicing Islam, deeply embellished with a pot & hashish habit, being beaten and battered by my son's father for no reason at all; although he called it love and respect. It was his plan to put fear in my heart because I was maturing and being noticed by real men. Note: (I'm step mother of 9 kids at age 18).

Next level rebellion; Introduced to cocaine & heroine at age 19. Well, the boy (heroine) was not my choice of drug, because I could be down by my darn self, but the girl (cocaine) was my candy, My BFF! I am the 80's version of an Annie Oakley gangster carrying a gun. I am riding dirty, and being beat frequently, until I just couldn't see, literally, nor take it anymore. I move back to Lawnside, NJ to my parents, with my son, to heal and get myself together. Well, this was really True Hell because, my father really drove the stake in me; drunk or sober. "You ain't nothing and never going to be nothing, what I tell you?" I found a job & my way back to Candy Girl, my BFF (cocaine) in NJ. The hatred escalated for my father so deeply, that it almost came to blows. Again, I couldn't take it anymore. I left for NY to start a new life with my cousins, but secretly bringing my craving for marijuana & habit for cocaine.

Y'all know it was no secret, but my parents didn't know. I left my son behind until I was able to get on my feet. New York was a BIG BIG mistake. My cousin had access to cocaine by the ounces. I quickly shacked & later married a sugar daddy, whom I later cheat on with a drug dealer. I send for my son and now start a real family, so I thought. I was a wife, a mother, going to college and working a job with a cocaine habit. They call this a functional addict, but we all know the functional becomes dysfunctional with any habit, until you hit rock bottom. My secret addiction got so bad, I sold to an undercover narcotics officer, and the next day the popo raided our home. They arrested my husband (house in his name) and found my smoking pipe (paraphernalia). The husband & I go to court for divorce settlement. I reveal I am 5 weeks pregnant with his child but in my mind know I cheated with the drug dealer (kingpin). The judge gives me my share & orders the future child support hearing. He leaves me to live with his new wife, I quit my job. I begin partying & tricking with the Kingpin. I start selling drugs (being my best customer) for him & became well known in the streets as "SiSi". I send my son back to my parents in NJ to protect him from the life his mother was now living (from 7-17yrs). I reveal to the kingpin that I am pregnant, who has a family and can't let this be known. I move to the other side of town (Hispanic) with enough drugs to go on my own and eventually, I become a Queenpin on the west side.

My water broke in the crack house and three weeks after the birth, I sent my daughter (Luvy) to my parents (from 3weeks – 10yrs).

Now, my secret is out. I'm partying & living amongst real drug addicts. I mean folks shooting heroin & cocaine (intravenously). Some had HIV. My queen pin reign was eventually dethroned, I was just like the rest; an addict. I was smoking my life away.

I began stealing from dealers & being on the run, hiding. Then, shoplifting and getting arrested with 7 aliases. Burned out of my home and almost trapped in a fire, jail became my front door. I was arrested & charged with the big Felony (possession of controlled substance with intent to sell) I was going to the Rackus Island in downstate NY. Facing 9-15yrs. It was then that I called on Jesus. I was given 1-3yrs parole with a six month drug boot camp sentence as given to first time felons & drug addicts. WOW, (pick your jaw up) Yep my thoughts exactly! Like Paul, It was there my relationship with Christ was rekindled. HE had Chosen a R.e.m.n.a.n.t! I went to Merriam Webster again for her definition of the word remnant. Let's not forget what chosen was defined as: An elect person or one who is the object of choice or divine favor.

Remnant: something that's left over once the rest is used up.

Survivor-"I made it!" Restored – be "Back Again!"

Let me reiterate, behind the abuse from disobedience, self-inflicted struggles, the bad choices, the vicious tricks of the enemy leaving me for broke or death, turning my back on God, deaf to his words and blind to his ways, but HE still had chosen me. Like Zion in Zechariah 8: 7; 11-13 God restored me.

HE took me back, again! He forgave me & blessed me with Favor.

[7] This is what the LORD Almighty says: "I will save my people from the countries of the east and the west. [8] I will bring them back to live in Jerusalem; they will be my people, and I will be faithful and righteous to them as their God."

[11] But now I will not deal with the remnant of this people as I did in the past," declares the LORD Almighty.

[12] "The seed will grow well, the vine will yield its fruit, the ground will produce its crops, and the heavens will drop their dew. I will give all these things as an inheritance to the remnant of this people. [13] Just as you, Judah and Israel, have been a curse among the nations, so I will save you, and you will be a blessing. Do not be afraid, but let your hands be strong." You may not have had the same down spiral, hit rock bottom, life experience that I had, but you're in or have been through a very bad storm. It is without question, that we may need a restructuring, a renovation, or an incredible makeover. Life has dealt us a bad hand. We've made the bad choices and the storms just keep coming. The more we have it our way and avoid the voice of God, the defeat endows us; mind body & soul. We are in it so deep the more we try to reach heaven the more hell we step into. We can't see our purpose, let alone fulfill it.

We forget whose we are? We isolate ourselves and become subject to our struggles. The enemy of depression takes over, failure encompasses the mind, and lack & worthlessness start making your agenda, our hearts become hardened because we have hurt or hindered our love ones, including God. We are so down & deep in the ways of the world, we can't nor want to hear from God. The blinders are on so tight, there is no glimpse of light in the peripheral vision.

Throwing our hands up- surrendering! Shaking our heads, losing hope & trust! The scream of frustration & defeat echoes "Whatever, just give up! You can't get it back! It's all over! Don't dream! You can't make it! You can't be healed! You are nothing to any one! You can't do this anymore! Just let it go!

STOP RIGHT THERE... YOU ARE A CHOSEN REMNANT!

So, here comes the blessing of impartation, a real life definition for the word REMNANT. It comes from my living testimony I just shared with you! Let me spell it out for you.

Remember- To be a Remnant is a privilege and an honor. Just like the old cliché "saving the best for last." Not only is a remnant a "Survivor"- I made it! It is being restored, "brought back again!" No matter where you are in life at this very moment, you are always Loved unconditionally by the Father, Protected by HIS Angels that have charge over you, because you're the chosen one to fulfill your purpose for the Kingdom of God. You have to dwell in the secret place of the Most High and you shall abide in the shadow of the almighty. Regardless, if we don't choose the least road of resistance, GOD's Gotcha! He will never leave you nor forsake You. Why you were not the first, nor will you be the last Chosen Remnant.

Micah 4:6-8 Living Bible (TLB)

[6] In that coming day, the Lord says that he will bring back his punished people—sick and lame and dispossessed— [7] and make them strong again in their own land, a mighty nation, and the Lord himself shall be their King from Mount Zion forever. [8] O Jerusalem—the Watchtower of God's people—your royal might and power will come back to you again, just as before.

Take a look in the mirror! You are God's Golden Child! Don't be tricked by the enemy or anyone that says 'you won't be anything.' Don't be deceived by comparing yourself to others and then feeling, I can't be used for the kingdom because…I don't have a degree, a bank account, an articulate voice, a bachelors, masters or doctrine degree, because I'm not light bright or because I have kinky hair. The Devil is a liar and ALWAYS will be. The next time you feel like God can't use you, just remember …

Noah was a drunk.

Abraham was too old.

Isaac was a daydreamer.

Jacob was a liar.

Leah was ugly.

Joseph was abused.

Moses had a stuttering problem.

Gideon was afraid.

Samson had long hair and was a womanizer.

Rahab was a prostitute.

Jeremiah and Timothy were too young.

David had an affair and was a murderer.

Elijah was suicidal.

Isaiah preached naked.

Jonah ran from God.

Naomi was a widow.

Job went bankrupt.

John the Baptist ate bugs.

Peter denied Christ.

The Disciples fell asleep while praying.

Martha worried about everything.

The Samaritan woman was divorced more than once.

Zacchaeus was too small.

Paul was too religious.

Timothy had an ulcer.

Lazarus was dead!

-Greg Laurie

Empowered- Because you are an Heir to the King, the likeness & image of GOD and as long as you are functioning like God (mindset and living by the principles of the Bible), you are empowered to Succeed. God's original intention is HIS final decision and so, here you are a winner by default!

Distraction is the first fierce tactic in conjunction with procrastination to deter you from your purpose, your visions, and your goals in life. If the enemy can get your focus off your purpose, you become subject to your struggles. Keep your eyes on the prize. If God is for you, who can be against you? Yes, Attitude is Altitude! It does determine how far you go in life. So, are you going to make up your mind and have an attitude of commitment? Any great accomplishment was manifested because of commitment. Commitment includes "The To Do, In spite of… attitude" and the transformed and renewed mind of Christ, not the El Mundo mind. We cannot have a double minded man, unstable in all our ways nature. This attitude or mindset is good for nothing or no one. You can't get caught up in your own devices. It definitely is no good for self because it only creates hardships, trials and tribulations. Doing 'ME' instead of 'JC' (Jesus Christ) is no good, so activate your VIP (Victory in Prayer) preventive maintenance system. God is limited by HIS own Word. It's important to understand that God's plans are not always for the NOW! HIS time is not our time, but HE is ALWAYS right on time.

Modify-Today! Right Now, is the time to make modifications to your daily routine and your daily lifestyle. Switch up the company you keep. Change your ambience. "Dare To Be Different." Be Bold, Brazen and Audacious in your relationship and trust in God. Stop listening to people, places & things that want to keep you stagnant in success. Don't get advice from wicked folks, nor stand around sinning folks or sit with mocking folks. Misery loves company. I'm sure you've heard this many times before, but make your haters your motivators. Bless them that curse you. As long as you know who you are in God, just keep it moving. "You are a giraffe and don't have time for turtles!" (TD Jakes, Instinct.) We have to be like Paul, "forget those things that are behind me and pressing forward to the things that are ahead." The plan of the enemy is to mess you up and he has a procedure to carry it out. His priority is to hinder your purpose and relationship with God by any and all means possible. Don't let people determine your destiny. Be aware of those who prophelie your future. Be very careful who you hook up with. People will bring you out just to get you caught up in something else.

Remove the blinders and recognize the pseudo people, places and things that will set you up for failure. Don't let dilemma or folks psych you out. Pray for wisdom and discernment daily.

Navigate- Set the GPS to 'Prosperity' as the Father predestined for you.

"For I know the plans I have for you declared the Lord, plans to prosper you and not to harm you, plans to give you hope and a future. Jeremiah 29:11

Dream Again! Write the vision down and make it plain. Don't allow distractions to deter you from your future. Don't allow anyone to sell you a dream, when you can save & buy your own. Our Father will meet You at the point of your needs. HIS mercy is inexhaustible. You can't ask for the Deep water blessing and live shallow water lives. You must go into the deep. Find your secret place & get intimate with the Father. It's that one on one quality time with Daddy that means everything. The enemy always tries to bind you and keep you caught up in mess and belittle you with constant mockery or flashbacks of failure. Make up your mind, what God's will is for your life. Seek HIM daily. If you do not know HIS will, ask him to reveal it to you. God must take precedent in your life. Do whatever it takes to Bounce Back! Pursue the path of simple faith. Prayer, Praise & Worship destroys your trials. You have to know where you are, not where it knows you are. Life and death are in the power of the tongue. God spoke IT into existence. Speak to your circumstances. You are an Heir to the same power.

Adhere to the 'Promises' to restore the remnant. "Instead of your shame you will receive a double portion, and instead of disgrace you will rejoice in your inheritance. And so you will inherit a double portion in your land, and everlasting joy will be yours. (Isaiah 61:7) The life of a believer is not at all a smooth operation. In fact it is totally opposite; because every new level of Faith brings a new level of devils. Our Lord and Savior Jesus Christ "paid it all." He conquered Hell for Us. All of our warfare, struggles, aches, pains, losses and failures, HE went through the trial and reigned in victory. We are here to be a living epistle and show gratitude for HIS sacrifice. No test, no testimony. Take your place to the throne and be ye ready to proclaim Christ! Tell the Devil to take a seat. You've got this by the blood of Jesus! God didn't give you the spirit of FEAR (**F**orget **E**verything **A**nd **R**un,) but Peace, Love and a Sound Mind! We must bounce back from what has bounced us around and set up camp to take it all back. You must be willing to cry (call on Jesus.) Be willing to try. (Be real about your goals & vision) Read, Study & Fast. Finally, you must be willing to die daily of the flesh. Wherever you laid down your Faith, Peace & Joy, "Go back & get it!"

Nourish the power of the Holy Spirit in your life. It is our source to restore inability.

Get intimate with the Holy Spirit and discover the fullness of God.

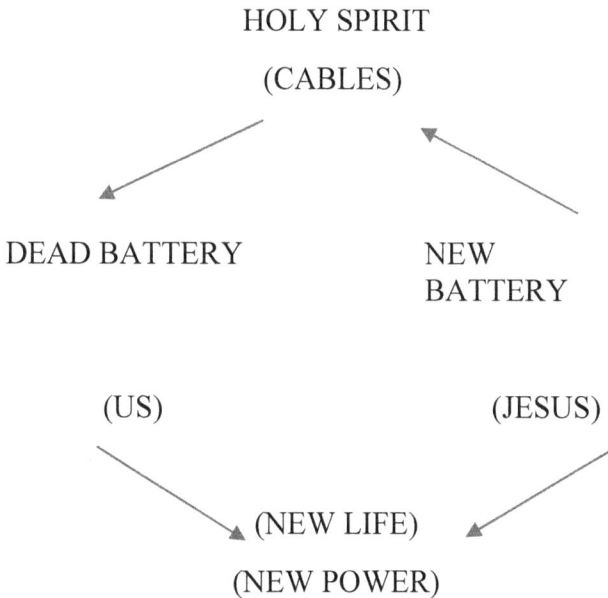

HOLY SPIRIT

(CABLES)

DEAD BATTERY   NEW BATTERY

(US)   (JESUS)

(NEW LIFE)

(NEW POWER)

Walk in the Spirit and you will not fulfill the lusts of the flesh. (Galatians 5:16) The flesh hinders your Spiritual life, and it doesn't want to release you from your old ways. Understand this, the WILL and the WORD of God is the Holy Spirit's job.

111

When we stay connected to God through the Holy Spirit, we walk in HIS power. It's all about the manifestation of the power that's within.

"Likewise the Holy Spirit also helps our infirmities: For we know not what we should pray for as we ought: But the Holy Spirit Himself makes intercession for us with groanings which cannot be uttered. 27 And God that searches the heart knows, what is the mind of the Holy Spirit, because the Holy Spirit makes intercession for the saints according to the will of God. 28 And we know that all things work together for good to them that love God, to them who are the called according to His purpose. 29 For whom He did foreknow, He also did predestinate to be conformed to the image of His Son."
ROMANS 8:26-29

Why am I not overcoming? I'm not walking in the Spirit. When we entertain the flesh, we hinder the spirit. But when we are in the Spirit, we produce fruit in our lives. In light of our defense, the Holy Spirit is our offense. The Holy Spirit is our guard listening for Jesus to give the play, so we can reach the goal line. Stand fast, because we are sealed with redemption; Activate resistance with the WORD of God; Hide the word in your heart; Spend time in prayer; Be obedient to the Spirit; and Reserve a place in your soul for you & God. When you Trust HIM, you will always have victory over your situation.

Testify- Go tell it on the mountains, over the hills and everywhere! Yes, you must go tell everyone that you were restored, and brought back because of God's grace & mercy! A Chosen Remnant. God never leaves Us, we leave him. I am so glad that HE loved me enough and led me back to salvation. Let me remind you, that being Saved is no excuse to keep falling. It's important to develop a spiritual sensitivity (Romans 12: 1-2) to be made whole. A closed mouth goes unfed. So, we must stay in constant communication with the Father in PRAYER! It's our connection to the power of God. Be still and hear from God. When you have regular conversations with God, In Jesus Name; You will always know his voice! Exercise your **FAITH** (**F**orever **A**m **I T**rusting **H**IM) God fulfills all requests in HIS time, because HE sees the total picture, when we just have a snapshot. God desires Us to be more than conquerors and to live as overcomers.

As I have shared with you my testimony, We must share yours with our fellow Brothers and Sisters. I hope you were blessed, delivered or restored back to God's unconditional Love for You. Today, I am so rich in Spirit! I'm Blessed beyond measure that I am a chosen remnant! Whew… Look at me NOW! So, don't hate on my glory, because you don't know my story!

I'm a Chosen Remnant … Favor is Fair!

I know not of tomorrow, I walk by faith today,

Tomorrow's in my Savior's hands and HE will lead the way.

If I should slip or struggle, my Savior's hand is there,

To stead me along my way, if life gets hard to bear.

And even if I trip and fall there's One who'll carry me,

So why then should I worry, when One loves me such as HE?

I know not of tomorrow, but of this I know for sure,

My Savior's there and HE does care and with HIM I'll endure.

When life starts to get you down, smile away that gloomy frown.

If you stumble now and then, get right up and start again.

You can have a sunny day, even if the clouds are grey,

It all depends upon your view, which way the world appears to you.

When you're tired of phony folks, check your wheels and mend your spokes.

Get your wagon rolling where your hearts are warm and people care.

Waste not hours, months and years on bitterness and foolish tears,

You're fashioned from a master plan, designed when God created man.

There's more to you than meets the eye, they only fail who never try,

Make your life a microscope to magnify each joy and hope.

Square your shoulders, lift your chin.

Toss your troubles to the wind,

And the Blessings you receive, even You will not believe.

A Chosen Remnant...Favor is Fair!

THE ACRONYM PAGE

These are just a few key inspirational Acronyms that are accompanied with the Word of God, because they were inspired by the Holy Spirit.

I pray you read and recall them to memory daily, to keep you rooted and grounded in Christ Jesus! Let it encourage you in a spiritual radical way to keep the enemy your footstool; Inspire you to birth your vision and expose your gift; Enhance the desire for more knowledge in your calling and increase your anointing. It is so in Jesus Name, Amen!

Y ield

E verything for

S alvation

2 Corinthians 1:20 NKJV - "For all the promises of God in Him are 'YES', and in Him Amen, to the glory of God through us."

Just say, "YES", to HIS way, YES to HIS will.

J esus

O perating in

Y ou

Nehemiah 8:10 NKJV - Then he said to them, "Go your way, eat the fat, drink the sweet, and send portions to those for whom nothing is prepared; for this day is holy to our Lord. Do not sorrow, for the JOY of the LORD is your strength."

Do NOT ever Surrender Your JOY, let alone allow the enemy to Steal it from You!

A llow the

S avior to

K eep You

John 14:14 NKJV - "If you ask anything in my name, I will do it."

Whatever you need, God's got it!

P eace &

R estoration

A re

Y ours

Psalm 55:17 KJV - "Evening and morning, and at noon, I will pray, and cry aloud: and HE will hear my voice."

Your prayers never fall on deaf ears. God the Father through his son Jesus Christ hears your voice and your request is made known. Believe when you pray and you will receive peace and restoration.

H olding

O n to my

P urpose

E ndowed within

Hebrews 6:19 AMP – "This hope (confident assurance) we have as an anchor of the soul (it cannot slip and it cannot break down under whatever pressure bears upon it) a safe and steadfast hope that enters within the veil (of the heavenly temple, the most Holy Place in which the very presence of God dwells."

You are a King's Kid born with a purpose and given power and dominion over your destiny. Walk in your Kingdom assignment with authority!

F aith

E xceeds

A ll things…

R ational /Irrational

Psalm 27:1 KJV- "The Lord is my light and my salvation; whom shall I fear? The Lord is the strength of my life; of whom shall I be afraid?"

Fear and Faith is like oil and water, they just don't mix. When you put your spiritual shades on, and step out in your full armor ensemble, your situation will smell the fresh emanation of your 'Victory.'

T ake

R efuge to

U tmost

S eek

T he Lord

Psalm 9: 10 KJV- "And they that know thy name will put their trust in thee: for thou, LORD, hast not forsaken them that seek thee."

There is Nobody like Jesus, and can't Nobody, do you like the Lord. Go deeper in your relationship with the LORD.

F ather

A ffirms

V ictory

O ver my

R amifications

Psalm 84:11 AMP- "For the Lord God is a sun and shield: The Lord bestows grace and favor and honor; No good thing will He withhold from those who walk uprightly."

Where there is Grace, You also get Mercy! These two benefits are the BEST guarantees you will ever receive in life. So, live right. Do right. Be right.

S ay

H ow

I

F eel

T oday

2Corinthian 5:17 NKJV- "Therefore, if anyone is in Christ, he is a new creation; old things have passed away; behold, all things have become new."

We will only get to the place God has divinely ordained us to be, after the Shift. The change or move of people, places & things; the renewing of our minds, the purging of our hearts and the freeing of our Souls, which comes by speaking it in daily prayer.

F orever

A m

I

T rusting

H im

James 1:17 AMP- "Every good thing given and every perfect gift is from above; it comes down from the Father of lights (the Creator and Sustainer of the heavens), in whom there is no variation (no rising or setting) or shadow cast by His turning (for He is perfect and never changes)."

It is a fact of life, that you are Royalty! Your inheritance is Infinite with Blessings, Power, Dominion and Authority. The grantor, Almighty Father is Greater than anything, anyone, anyplace that the enemy would use to distract or detour the grantee, You from being GREATNESS!

P redestined

R estoration

A ssured

I ntercession

S upplications

E mphasized

I Peter 2:9 NKJV- "But you are a chosen generation, a royal priesthood, a holy nation, and HIS own special people, that you may proclaim the praises of Him who called you out of the darkness into HIS marvelous light.

One thing I know for sure, and that is; 'There is Power in your Praise! It's the war chant of Victory, and the enemy is immediately defeated that is the reason he tries so hard to shut your mouth. Make a joyful noise unto the Lord, and watch your Peace be restored, your Strength be renewed, and your Joy returned.

P ray

U ntil

S omething

H appens

   And

P raise

U ntil the

L ord

L ets it go

James 5:13 AMP- "Is anyone among you suffering? He must pray. Is anyone joyful? He is to sing praises (to God)"

There is a lesson to be a more authentic communicator; "say what you mean; mean what you say." This holds true when we pray and believe. We push our prayer (say what we mean) and we pull after the prayer (mean what we say) in faith. Testimony Time!

B ecause

L ord, you

E stablish

S piritual

S plendor

E very

D ay

Numbers 6:24-26 KJV- "The Lord bless thee, and keep thee: The Lord make his face shine upon thee, and be gracious unto thee: The Lord lift up his countenance upon thee, and give thee peace."

When you are Blessed by the Best, Never mind the Rest; it doesn't even matter!

S alvation

O ffered

U niting to

L ord Jesus Christ.

W ashed

I niquities.

N o more

N ostalgia.

I mmediate

N ewness of

G race

Matthew 28:19 NLT- "Therefore, go and make disciples of all the nations, baptizing them in the name of the Father and the Son and the Holy Spirit."

This is the reason God gave his only begotten Son, Jesus Christ to die for our sins and rise again with ALL power in his hands. We are the Body of Christ, with a commandment to help one another not perish to the ways of the world. We must be ready, beautiful and have lived a fruitful life when Jesus Christ returns for his Bride, Us the Church.

APPENDIX

WWW. BIBLEGATEWAY.COM (AMP, MESSAGE & NKJV)

THE DAILY BREAD

EXPOSITION COMMENTARIES

WWW.BIBLEMEANINGS.INFO

DR..RICK EZELL- LIFE WAY CHRISTIAN RESOURCES

SOUNDS OF BLACKNESS

MANTIS TILLERS WEBSITE

RAPTURE NOTES & KEITH KERRIN

QUOTES BY JFK

LAYMANS BIBLE ENCYCLOPEDIA

HOLMAN REFERENCE DICTIONARY CONCORDANCE

THE COMPLETE JEWISH BIBLE

BASIC THEOLOGY- CHARLES RYRIE

WIKIPEDIA

DISCIPLECHRISTIAN.COM

BLUE LETTER BOOK BIBLE

GLOBALPRAYER.COM- THE EXPOSITORY OUTLINE SERIES: THE BOOK OF THE PSALMS

WIKI DIFF

GINA LAURIN- I'LL ENDURE

LORE DOREMUS BIEBER- BLESSINGS EVERYWHERE

PSYBLOG – DR PELIN KESEBIR

The Acronym Preacher~ Dr. Cindy

Kingdom Experience

Native of Port of Spain, Trinidad, 'Rev' Cindy Bailey was adopted & grew up in Philadelphia, Pa & Lawnside, NJ (oldest historical black community in So Jersey.) Her father was Ex-Army and her mother was a Real Estate clerk for a Jewish multi-millionaire that later became her God-Father. Rev Bailey was raised an only child pretty much by her Grandmother Ruth, who taught her how to be a module Entrepreneur with multiple incomes, and the Evangelist that she is today. Her grandmother fed people, clothed people, gave them lodging, jobs and cared for all children. She read her Word and supported many churches. She visited hospitals, prisons and nursing homes. She attended and paid for funerals. She held block parties and had the respect of every drug dealer, motorcycle gang leader, Black mafia, Italian mafia, and politician. There was nothing and no one that could separate her Grandmother Ruth from serving and helping God's people and nor was she afraid to go anywhere to decree "Thus says the Lord!"

"Rev' Cindy Bailey has been working in the community serving the Kingdom of God instilled by her Grandmother.
Her passion and heart to serve is tireless. She has been awarded Certificates of Appreciation from various Ministries & organizations; "Western NY Humanity Award" (2000-2003); Community Outreach Achiever (2000-2003) where she was given the name" The Street General"; and most recently recipient of the Presidential Lifetime Achiever's Award 2016.

Rev Bailey is the President of K I N International Ministry Inc. (Kingdom Intercessors Network) that partners & supports over 50 ministries (food, shelter, housing, transportation, building life centers, orphanages, churches, schools) locally and throughout the nation. She organizes Community Outreach events that feed 100's of families, provides education resources, housing resources, health resources, employment resources and business growth with major vendor opportunities;

Empowerment & Marketplace Summits & Motivational Conferences. Rev Bailey travels throughout the towns, cities, countries and continents speaking, preaching and teaching a Rema word of God. Her ultimate Vision is to help homeless people reconnect with their Gifts and talents. She wants to help them build self- confidence and develop a renewed relationship with God and their Families. Serving as Outreach Director for her current Church, Mt. Sinai Baptist Church, under leadership of Bishop Dr. David E Jackson (Author of Work Your Room), she travels globally doing Missionary work.

Professional Experience

"Rev" Cindy Bailey is a Financial Specialist that has worked in the Banking, Insurance, Real Estate, Construction, Manufacturing industries for over 16 years. She has held positions as Controller, Corporate Accounting Manager or Staff Accountant in Major Fortune 500 & Big 4 Industries like HSBC Bank, Axis Insurance Company, Pilgrim Village Brokers, Waste Management just to name a few. She is currently a Controller for major International Manufacturing Company in lieu of being a Business Entrepreneur: THKUGSUS LLC (Thank You Jesus) specializing in Finances that includes services: Tax Preparation (ERO), Audits, Credit Repair, Payroll, Accounting, Bookkeeping, Business Consulting, QuickBooks Training, Notary and top of the line, teaching "Stewardship Based on God's Principles."

She is certified in various Accounting, Insurance & Manufacturing software qualified to Train & Teach.

Affiliated & Member of: AICPCU: American Institute for Chartered Property Casualty Underwriters, AIPB: American Institute of Professional Bookkeepers, NACPB: National Association Certified Public Bookkeepers, NARTP: National Association of Registered Tax Return Preparers, NNA: National Notary Association, and QB ProAdvisor Member. Board Treasury Member of Impact Center Georgia; Board Member of For His Glory Christian Center; CFO of MYB By Me Inc. Construction; Business Associate of Show It Entertainment Inc., Marketing PR Specialist for DE Jackson Enterprise.

Education

Graduate of Sterling High School, Stratford, NJ-College Prep; Erie County Community College, Buffalo, NY- Accounting; University at Buffalo (EEOC)-Business Computer Technology; Center for Financial Institute, Buffalo, NY- Banking Operations, AAS; Alameda College, Alameda, CA- BBA, Major in Finance; Emory University-Grant Writer Certification; Western NY COGIC Seminary, Project Ephesus Campus/District1- MDiv; Fellowship International School of Ministry & Bible College, Metaire,LA- DMin.

World Travels

Dominican Republic- Puerto Playa, Santiago
Italy-Rome, Florence, Milan
France-Paris
Caribbean: St. Lucia, St. Martinique,
St. Maarten, St. Kitts, Jamaica, Grenada
Grand Turks, Caicos, St. Thomas
Portugal
Spain- Barcelona
Turkey- Istanbul
Africa-Ghana, Accra
Canada
United States- 28 of 50 states including Puerto Rico

Partial Speaking List

First Baptist Church of Garmon St, Warner Robins, GA
For His Glory Christian Center, Warner Robins, GA
Shekinah Glory Praise & Worship Center, Warner Robins, GA
Disciples of Faith Holiness Church, Atlanta, Ga
New Beginnings Women's Ministry, Talladega, AL
A Gathering of the Generals, Atlanta, GA
Mt. Sinai Baptist Church, Atlanta, GA
First Gethsemane Baptist Church, Atlanta, GA
New Beginnings Baptist Church of East Atlanta, Atlanta, GA
Light of the World International Ministry, Stockbridge, GA
Wings of Prayer Ministry, Walterboro, SC
Sister to Sister Healing, Atlanta, GA
Out of the Box Ministries, Atlanta, GA
Women With a Mission Sisterhood, Orange Beach, AL
Love in Action Community Outreach, Jonesboro, GA
Promise Faith Church Auditorium, Sakaman, Blue-Lagoon, Accra
Positive Life Chapel International, Accra
Harvest Christian Fellowship Church, Fort Worth, Texas
Once Broken New Life Inc., Douglasville, GA
Life Changes Church, Douglasville, GA

Book 'Rev' Cindy Bailey

Email: **kinginternet.international@yahoo.com**
thkugsus@yahoo.com

Call: 404-717-2824
Website(s): **www.thkugsus.com**
www.kininternationalministry.org